Second Workshop on Corpus Generation and Corpus Augmentation for Machine Translation (CoCo4MT 2023)

Macau, China
5 September 2023

ISBN: 978-1-7138-9038-6

Printed from e-media with permission by:

Curran Associates, Inc.
57 Morehouse Lane
Red Hook, NY 12571

CURRAN ASSOCIATES INC.
proceedings
.com

Some format issues inherent in the e-media version may also appear in this print version.

Association for Computational Linguistics
209 N. Eighth Street
Stroudsburg, Pennsylvania 18360

Phone: 1-570-476-8006
Fax: 1-570-476-0860

acl@aclweb.org

Additional copies of this publication are available from:

Curran Associates, Inc.
57 Morehouse Lane
Red Hook, NY 12571 USA
Phone: 845-758-0400
Fax: 845-758-2633
Email: curran@proceedings.com
Web: www.proceedings.com

CoCo4MT 2023

MTS Machine Translation Summit 2023

September 4-8, 2023 Macau SAR, China

Proceedings of the Second Workshop on Corpus Generation and Corpus Augmentation for Machine Translation

September 5, 2023

Aim of the workshop

In this second version of the workshop on corpus generation and corpus augmentation for machine translation (CoCo4MT 2023), we attempt to further establish augmentation techniques that can be used for machine translation, especially in low-resource settings. Due to the overwhelming success with a variety of languages in CoCo4MT 2022[1], in this CoCo4MT workshop we further introduce unique low-resource languages like Urdi, Bengali, and Icelandic. Additionally, new machine learning techniques that based on segmentation, data mining, and deep learning are presented. As an extra addition, this year we introduce a shared task for the first time that focuses on the construction of corpora for machine translation.

The CoCo4MT 2023 submissions provide open source access to their code and corpus which is found directly in each submission. The CoCo4MT 2023 website[2] is available publicly. It contains all of the information for the previous year along with this year's workshop.

[1] Ortega, J. E., Carpuat, M., Chen, W., Kann, K., Lignos, C., Popovic, M., and Tafreshi, S., editors (2022). *Proceedings of the 15th biennial conference of the Association for Machine Translation in the Americas (Workshop 2: Corpus Generation and Corpus Augmentation for Machine Translation).* Association for Machine Translation in the Americas.

[2] `https://sites.google.com/view/coco4mt`

Workshop scope and details

It is a well-known fact that machine translation systems, especially those that use deep learning, require massive amounts of data. Several resources for languages are not available in their human-created format. Some of the types of resources available are monolingual, multilingual, translation memories, and lexicons. Those types of resources are generally created for formal purposes such as parliamentary collections when parallel and more informal situations when monolingual. The quality and abundance of resources including corpora used for formal reasons is generally higher than those used for informal purposes. Additionally, corpora for low-resource languages, languages with less digital resources available, tends to be less abundant and of lower quality.

CoCo4MT is a workshop centered around research that focuses on manual and automatic corpus creation, cleansing, and augmentation techniques specifically for machine translation. We accept work that covers any language (including sign language) but we are specifically interested in those submissions that explici tly report on work with languages with limited existing resources (low-resource languages). Since techniques from high-resource languages are generally statistical in nature and could be used as generic solutions for any language, we welcome submissions on high-resource languages also.

CoCo4MT aims to encourage research on new and undiscovered techniques. We hope that the methods presented at this workshop will lead to the development of high-quality corpora that will in turn lead to high-performing MT systems and new dataset creation for multiple corpora. We hope that submissions will provide high-quality corpora that are available publicly for download and can be used to increase machine translation performance thus encouraging new dataset creation for multiple languages that will, in turn, provide a general workshop to consult for corpora needs in the future. The workshop's success will be measured by the following key performance indicators:

- Promotes the ongoing increase in quality of machine translation systems when measured by standard measurements,
- Provides a meeting place for collaboration from several research areas to increase the availability of commonly used corpora and new corpora,
- Drives innovation to address the need for higher quality and abundance of low-resource language data.

Topics of the workshop include but are not limited to:

- Difficulties with using existing corpora (e.g., political considerations or domain limitations) and their effects on final MT systems,
- Strategies for collecting new MT datasets (e.g., via crowdsourcing),
- Data augmentation techniques,
- Data cleansing and denoising techniques,
- Quality control strategies for MT data,
- Exploration of datasets for pretraining or auxiliary tasks for training MT systems.

This year, we also conducted the first CoCo4MT shared task, where we invited participants to develop and share their methods on identifying beneficial instances for machine translation without any existing parallel data in a target language. The goal of the shared task was to encourage research on making the data curation process for machine translation more efficient, particularly for low-resource languages where collecting data to train high-performing MT systems is constrained by cost and scale. We used multi-way parallel data from the Bible to create training and evaluation data in nine languages, which are publicly available here: `https://github.com/ananyaganesh/coco4mt-shared-task`. We received two submissions to the shared task, and the details of both systems are published as part of the proceedings, along with the findings of the shared task.

Invited Speakers (listed alphabetically by first name)

We are happy our dear colleagues Jack Halpern, Manuel Mager, and Marta R. Costa-jussà have prepared talks on three important topics for CoCo4MT 2023.

Jack Halpern, The CJK Dictionary Institute

Jack Halpern, CEO of The CJK Dictionary Institute, is a lexicographer by profession. For sixteen years was engaged in the compilation of the New Japanese-English Character Dictionary, and as a research fellow at Showa Women's University (Tokyo), he was editor-in-chief of several kanji dictionaries for learners, which have become standard reference works. Jack Halpern, who has lived in Japan over 40 years, was born in Germany and has lived in six countries including France, Brazil, Japan, and the United States. An avid polyglot who specializes in Japanese and Chinese lexicography, he has studied 18 languages (speaks ten fluently) and has devoted several decades to the study of linguistics and lexicography. On a lighter note, Jack Halpern loves the sport of unicycling. Founder and long-time president of the International Unicycling Federation, he has promoted the sport worldwide and is a director of the Japan Unicycling Association. Currently, his passions are playing the quena and improving his Chinese, Esperanto, and Arabic.

Marta R. Costa-jussà, Meta AI

Marta R. Costa-jussà is a research scientist at Meta AI since February 2022. She received her PhD from the UPC in 2008. Her research experience is mainly in Machine Translation. She has worked at LIMSI-CNRS (Paris), Barcelona Media Innovation Center, Universidade de São Paulo, Institute for Infocomm Research (Singapore), Instituto Politécnico Nacional (Mexico), the University of Edinburgh and at Universitat Politècnica de Catalunya (UPC, Barcelona), co-leading the MT-UPC Group. She has participated in 18 European/Spanish research projects; she has organised 12 workshops in top venues and she has published more than 100 papers. She has been part of the Editorial Board of the Computer Speech and Language journal. She has received an ERC Starting Grant and two Google Faculty Research Awards (2018 and 2019).

Manuel Mager, AWS AI Labs

Manuel Mager is an Applied Scientist at AWS AI Labs, and completing his Ph.D. candidate at the University of Stuttgart, Germany. He graduated in informatics from the National Autonomous University of Mexico (UNAM) and did a Master's in Computer Science at the Metropolitan Autonomous University, Mexico (UAM). His research is focused on Natural Language Processing for low resource languages, mainly indigenous languages of the American continent that are polysynthetic. He also worked on Graph-to-text generation and information extraction.

Other speakers and guests Due to its previous success, CoCo4MT will once again host a panel that includes several other researchers and notable speakers. The panel speakers will be announced in a future (post-edited) version of the proceedings.

Organizers

John E. Ortega, Northeastern University
Marine Carpuat, University of Maryland
William Chen, Carnegie Mellon University
Ananya Ganesh, University of Colorado Boulder
Katharina Kann, University of Colorado Boulder
Constantine Lignos, Brandeis University
Jonne Saleva, Brandeis University
Shabnam Tafreshi, University of Maryland
Rodolfo Zevallo, Universitat Pompeu Fabra

Program Committee (listed alphabetically by first name)

Abteen Ebrahimi, University of Colorado Boulder
Ananya Ganesh, University of Colorado Boulder
Bharathi Raja Chakravarthi, National University of Ireland Galway
Bonaventure F. P. Dossou, McGill University
Constantine Lignos, Brandeis University
Flammie Pirinen, UiT Norgga árktalaš universitehta
Jasper Kyle Catapang, University of Birmingham
John E. Ortega, Northeastern University
Jonne Sälevä, Brandeis University
Katharina Kann, University of Colorado Boulder
Kochiro Watanabe, The University of Tokyo
Koel Dutta Chowdhury, Saarland University
Majid Latifi, University of York
Maria Art Antonette Clariño, University of the Philippines Los Baños
Marine Carpuat, University of Maryland
Miquel Esplà-Gomis, Universitat d'Alacant
Pablo Gamallo, University of Santiago de Compostela - CITIUS
Patrick Simianer, Lilt
Rico Sennrich, University of Zurich
Rodolfo Zevallos, Universitat Pompeu Fabra
Sangjee Dondrub, Qinghai Normal University
Santanu Pal, Wipro
Shabnam Tafreshi, University of Maryland
Shiran Dudy, Northeastern University
Surafel Melaku Lakew, Amazon
Thepchai Supnithi, National Electronics and Computer Technology Center
William Chen, Carnegie Mellon University

Table of Contents

Workshop Program

Do Not Discard – Extracting Useful Fragments from Low-Quality Parallel Data to Improve Machine Translation

Steinþór Steingrímsson steinthor18@ru.is
Department of Computer Science, Reykjavik University, Iceland

Pintu Lohar pintu.lohar@adaptcentre.ie
ADAPT Centre, School of Computing, Dublin City University, Ireland

Hrafn Loftsson hrafn@ru.is
Department of Computer Science, Reykjavik University, Iceland

Andy Way andy.way@adaptcentre.ie
ADAPT Centre, School of Computing, Dublin City University, Ireland

Abstract

When parallel corpora are preprocessed for machine translation (MT) training, a part of the parallel data is commonly discarded and deemed non-parallel due to odd-length ratio, overlapping text in source and target sentences or failing some other form of a semantic equivalency test. For language pairs with limited parallel resources, this can be costly as in such cases modest amounts of acceptable data may be useful to help build MT systems that generate higher quality translations. In this paper, we refine parallel corpora for two language pairs, English–Bengali and English–Icelandic, by extracting sub-sentence fragments from sentence pairs that would otherwise have been discarded, in order to increase recall when compiling training data. We find that by including the fragments, translation quality of NMT systems trained on the data improves significantly when translating from English to Bengali and from English to Icelandic.

1 Introduction

Neural Machine Translation (NMT) usually exhibits good performance when trained on a large amount of good-quality bilingual sentence pairs. However, developing a good-quality NMT system for language pairs with limited resources is a challenging task. When compiling a parallel corpus, and during preprocessing for training, a significant amount of sentence pairs are commonly discarded before the data can be used to train the translation model. That may not be much of a problem for high-resource language pairs, where the training data contains sufficiently large number of sentence pairs even after discarding many of them, but language pairs with limited resources can be negatively impacted if the filtering is inaccurate, as less training data may limit the quality of the translation model.

The first stage of NMT training involves preprocessing the training data in which the text pairs go through several steps such as tokenising, filtering and byte-pair encoding (Sennrich et al., 2016). In the filtering step, all the text pairs with unusual source-target sentence-length

Proceedings of the Second Workshop on Corpus Generation and Corpus Augmentation for Machine Translation, pages 1–13
September 5, 2023, Macau SAR, China.

ratio, extremely long sentences, absence of text for either one of the languages, or other anomalies are discarded. These can be a substantial percentage of available parallel pairs, and for language pairs that have limited resources, a number which could affect performance noticeably. Although the sentence pairs are discarded due to irregularities that can be detrimental for MT systems, they often contain a considerable amount of semantically similar segment pairs at the phrase, chunk or sub-sentence level. For example, if a source-language sentence contains 50 words and its target counterpart contains 10 words, they are likely to be discarded due to odd sentence-length ratio. However, they may contain similar information and some equivalent phrases or segments. This leads us to the two research questions we seek to answer in this paper:

1. **Can deficient training data for MT be identified and refined to be more useful?**
2. **Can data commonly discarded, when compiling or pre-processing training sets for NMT, be mined for parallel sentence pairs beneficial for training?**

In order to seek answers to these questions, we conduct two experiments. In the first one, described in Section 4, we work with English–Bengali sentence pairs from the *Samanantar* parallel corpus (Ramesh et al., 2022). We score the pairs and select a subset of the highest scoring pairs for training. The discarded sentences are then divided into subsentences and treated as a comparable corpus, which we mine for sentence pairs acceptable for training. In our second experiment, described in Section 5, we work with a subcorpus of the English–Icelandic parallel corpus *ParIce* (Barkarson and Steingrímsson, 2019), which is composed of a collection of parallel texts in a number of domains. The subcorpus we work with contains regulations and other documents published in relations with the EEA agreement. We collect all sentences that did not obtain alignments during the alignment process, as well as sentence pairs filtered out due to insufficient quality. We treat these discarded sentences as we treated the English–Bengali data, i.e. divide the sentences into subsentences and mine them for sentence pairs potentially useful for MT training.

Finally, we train multiple NMT models to assess the feasibility of the approach. Our evaluation shows that MT quality can be increased by extracting useful chunks at a sub-sentence level from data that would usually be discarded.

2 Related Work

A significant amount of research has been carried out in the area of exploiting comparable corpora for MT. Karimi et al. (2018) extracted parallel sentences from Wikipedia documents by translating documents in Persian into English, and also in the reverse direction, to extract semantically equivalent sentence pairs. Steingrímsson et al. (2021b) employed three different measures to identify and score parallel sentences from comparable corpora for English–Icelandic: Crosslingual information retrieval (CLIR) based approach (Lohar et al., 2016), LaBSE, and WAScore, a word alignment based scoring mechanism introduced in the paper. Ramesh et al. (2022) extracted parallel sentences from the web by using:

- monolingual corpora crawled from web,
- OCR to extract sentences from scanned documents,
- multilingual representation models for sentence alignment, and
- nearest neighbor searching method.

Munteanu and Marcu (2006) experimented with extracting parallel sub-sentences from comparable corpora using word alignments to link words in the source and target language and calculate a signal value to estimate the probability of all word to word links, which they use to determine if two strings of words are parallel. Other work on sub-sentential fragment extraction include Hangya and Fraser (2019), who used bilingual word embeddings to greedily align words in partly parallel sentences, and then average the word alignment scores and weigh them using segment length to decide if a given segment pair is parallel. However, we are not aware of any work till date attempting to utilize discarded parallel training data.

Recent work on developing English–Bengali MT systems include Bal et al. (2019), who proposed approaches for translating assertive, interrogative and imperative English sentences into Bengali by analysing their sentence patterns and using different Bengali grammatical rules. Paul and Purkhyastha (2020) developed an English–Bengali NMT system for the aviation domain trained on a unique English–Bengali parallel corpus in this domain. Siddique et al. (2020) built a translation system using an encoder-decoder recurrent neural network with the help of knowledge-based context vectors for mapping English and Bengali words.

Until recently, work on English–Icelandic MT was limited to an Apertium (Forcada et al., 2011) based model (Brandt et al., 2011). The ParIce corpus was published in 2018, spurring work using statistical and neural methods for English–Icelandic MT. Jónsson et al. (2020) presented the first published work on Phrase-Based Statistical MT (PBSMT) and NMT for Icelandic and, in 2021, English–Icelandic was one of the language pairs in the shared news translation task at WMT (Akhbardeh et al., 2021).

3 Methodology and Experiments

In this work, we reexamine discarded parallel training data by segmenting it and extracting semantically equivalent bilingual segments. We then utilise parallel segments extracted from the discarded data as additional parallel training data if it can be deduced from our methods that the segments will be useful for MT training. We compare the quality of the translation output to baseline models. In the case of English–Bengali, the comparison is made to a model trained on the full Samanantar corpus and to the state-of-the-art IndicTrans model (Ramesh et al., 2022), and in the case of English–Icelandic, to a model trained on the aligned and filtered corpus, without the sentence pairs mined from discarded data.

3.1 Datasets

For our first experiments, we re-evaluate English–Bengali parallel sentence pairs from the *Samanantar* corpus (Ramesh et al., 2022), the largest publicly available parallel corpora collection for 11 Indic languages. The original English–Bengali parallel training data contains 8.52 million sentence pairs, sufficiently large for NMT training. However, when inspecting random samples from the dataset, we found that not all the sentence pairs are mutual translations, although many contain parallel sub-sentences that can be useful to acquire translation knowledge.

For our second experiment, we use the raw parallel documents used to compile the EEA subcorpus of ParIce (Barkarson and Steingrímsson, 2019), obtained from the corpus publisher. We took aside $903,692$ sentence pairs that had been aligned and accepted after filtering. We then collected all other sentences in the corpus, which had been discarded at some stage in the compilation process. Some did not obtain an alignment by the sentence alignment algorithm while others were not accepted by filters. In total, this resulted in over $833K$ discarded sentences in English and over $927K$ sentences in Icelandic.

3.2 Training and evaluation

For both language pairs (English–Bengali and English–Icelandic), we train separate NMT models for both translation directions. Fairseq (Ott et al., 2019) is used to train Transformer$_{BASE}$ models, as described in Vaswani et al. (2017), except that we use byte-pair encoding with a

```
--arch transformer
--share-all-embeddings
--dropout 0.2
--label-smoothing 0.2
--criterion label smoothed cross entropy
--weight-decay 0.0001
--optimizer adam
--adam-betas '(0.9, 0.98)'
--clip-norm 0
--lr-scheduler inverse sqrt
--warmup-updates 4000
--warmup-init-lr 1e-7
--keep-last-epochs 5
--patience 5
--skip-invalid-size-inputs-valid-test
--lr 0.0005 --stop-min-lr 1e-9
--max-tokens 16000
--fp16
```

Figure 1: Hyperparameters for all trained models.

shared vocabulary size of $32K$ and set dropout to 0.2, in line with Sennrich and Zhang (2019) whose results indicate that a more aggressive dropout than applied in the original Transformer paper leads to higher BLEU scores in low and medium resource settings. We train each model on a single A100 GPU with early stopping on validation loss with the patience set to 5 epochs, using the same setup as Ramesh et al. (2022) when they trained Transformer$_{BASE}$ models to compare against their large model. For validation we use the FLORES development set (Goyal et al., 2022) for English–Bengali and the in-domain EEA development set from the ParIce 21.10 dev/test splits (Barkarson et al., 2021), compiled from held-out documents from the same source as the ParIce corpus. All our hyperparameters are given in Figure 1.

We evaluate the models automatically using BLEU scores (Papineni et al., 2002), using the test sentences from the same datasets we used for validation. We calculate the scores using SacreBLEU (Post, 2018), for them to be reproducible and comparable. For Bengali–English, we follow the process carried out by (Ramesh et al., 2022). We use the default mteval-v12a tokenizer, but, since the SacreBLEU tokenizer does not support Bengali, we first tokenize using the IndicNLP[1] tokenizer before running SacreBLEU. SacreBLEU signatures for en→bn[2], bn→en[3] and for en→is and is→en[4] are provided in footnotes.

4 Refining an English–Bengali Corpus

We begin by calculating similarity scores for each of the $8.52M$ English–Bengali sentence pairs in the Samanantar corpus. We use LASER (Artetxe and Schwenk, 2019), LaBSE, and WAScore (Steingrímsson et al., 2021b) for scoring the sentence pairs. LASER uses a pre-trained BiLSTM encoder trained on data in 93 languages to generate scores for sentence pairs. LaBSE uses dual encoder models, with the encoding architecture following the BERT Base model, and additive margin softmax which creates a large margin around positive pairs. WAScore is word alignment based and uses CombAlign (Steingrímsson et al., 2021a), which again employs multiple word aligners to arrive at accurate word alignments. In order to remove sentences most likely to be deficient, we treat this as a candidate list extracted from comparable corpora, following the methodology described in Steingrímsson et al. (2021b), using a logistic regression classifier

[1] `https://github.com/AI4Bharat/indicnlp_catalog`
[2] SacreBLEU signature: BLEU+numrefs.1+case.mixed+tok.none+smooth.exp+version.2.2.0
[3] SacreBLEU signature: BLEU+numrefs.1+case.mixed+tok.13a+smooth.exp+version.2.2.0
[4] SacreBLEU signature: BLEU+numrefs.1+case.mixed+tok.13a+smooth.exp+version.2.2.0

Dataset	Size (#sentence pairs $\times 10^6$)	en→bn BLEU	en→bn time	bn→en BLEU	bn→en time
Samanantar	8.52	18.1	29h27m	27.9	20h2m
S_1	5.6	19.0	14h33m	27.8	19h5m
S_2	5	19.1	15h43m	***28.5***	11h22m
S_3	4	18.9	16h32m	27.2	9h8m
S_4	3	**19.5**	7h32m	26.6	6h38m
S_5	2	18.7	5h57m	25.6	5h37m
S_6	1	17.3	1h29m	23.3	1h43m
S_7	0.5	14.9	1h6m	19.9	37m

Table 1: BLEU score for models trained on different sets of sub-selected English–Bengali data until convergence. Scores in bold are highest and significantly higher than other scores according to a bootstrap resampling test.

that considers all three scores to decide which sentence pairs to filter out. We then order the remaining sentence pairs based on LaBSE similarity score and create differently sized sets of parallel sentence pairs, with one set containing the 500 thousand highest scoring pairs (S_7), another containing the 1 million highest scoring pairs (S_6), and so on. Table 1 shows the size of the original data set and the different sets of selected data. Note that the S_1 data set represents all the 5.6 million sentence pairs that our rather lenient classifier deemed acceptable. The other sets contain a subset of the sentence pairs in S_1, as described above.

4.1 Baseline

We trained models for both translation directions on the full Samanantar dataset of $8.5M$ sentence pairs and set that as a baseline for our experiment. The models achieved 18.1 and 27.9 BLEU for en→bn and bn→en respectively (see Table 1), which is somewhat below the scores of 20.3 and 32.2 reported for IndicTrans (Ramesh et al., 2022), trained on the same data. This difference may be explained by the model size. We train Transformer$_{BASE}$ models with ≈60M parameters, while IndicTrans is a very large transformer model with ≈400M parameters.

4.2 Segment pairs for similarity measurement

We evaluate and compare the models trained on different amounts of data, with the smallest datasets having the highest scoring sentence pairs in terms of the similarity score used, and find that the BLEU score rises when sentence pairs are added, but only up to a point, when it starts

Language	Original sentence	Segments after splitting
Bengali	রাজনৈতিক শক্তি ও সামরিক বাহিনীর সম্পর্ক বিষয়ে তিনি বলেন, সরকারের উচিৎ আর্মির সঙ্গে ভালো ও সামঞ্জস্যপূর্ণ সম্পর্ক বজায় রাখা।	1. রাজনৈতিক শক্তি 2. সামরিক বাহিনীর সম্পর্ক বিষয়ে তিনি বলেন 3. সরকারের উচিৎ আর্মির সঙ্গে ভালো 4. সামঞ্জস্যপূর্ণ সম্পর্ক বজায় রাখা
English	Solvents can be gasses, liquids, or solids.	1. Solvents can be gasses 2. liquids 3. solids

Figure 2: English and Bengali segments after splitting.

Type of selection/discarding	**#sentence/segment pairs**
Whole pairs selected	$1.2M$
Whole Bengali and Partial English	$79K$
Whole English and Partial Bengali	$88K$
Both partial	$456K$
Discarded	$1.7M$

Table 2: Result of sub-sentential selection

going down again (see Table 1). These turning points are different for each language direction. Steingrímsson et al. (2023) show that different filtering approaches may suit different translation directions, even when working with the same parallel corpus. They speculate that this may be due to lower quality text in one language than in the other, affecting the quality of translations into that language if no special effort is put into filtering these lower quality texts out especially. More complex morphology in one language, effects of translationese or other systemic factors may also play a role. In our work, while evaluating our approaches on both language directions, we aim our data selection on translating from English and into Bengali and Icelandic.

When evaluating the Samanantar subsets, shown in Table 1, the turning point is lower for the en$\rightarrow$bn dataset, with the highest BLEU for a subset of $3M$ sentence pairs. As we do not know whether a more fine grained turning point would be below or above the $3M$ sentence pair mark, to err on the side of caution we use the $2M$ highest scoring sentence pairs as a foundation for our final system, and investigate further all the other $3.6M$ pairs from the set of $5.6M$ approved by our classifier. We generate sub-sentential segments for each of these sentences and use comparable corpora mining approaches to find optimal sentence pairs. For that we first split up the sentences in both languages using commas and conjunctions as delimiters. In English we use "and" and "or", and "ও" and "এবং" in Bengali. Figure 2 shows examples of how the sentences can be split. From the segments we generate all possible combinations of up to six adjoining sentence parts for each language. We then pair each segment combination against all segment combinations in the other language for any given pair. This results in a total of $\approx$115 million pairs to be evaluated, representing the $3.6M$ sentence pairs from the parallel corpus.

We use LaBSE to estimate semantic similarity for all segment pairs. Feng et al. (2022) use the threshold 0.6 for selecting sentence pairs mined from CommonCrawl,[5] as they find pairs scoring higher than or equal to this threshold likely to be at least partial translations of each other. Partial translations are often an effect of misalignment and according to Koehn et al. (2018) including them in a training set can be detrimental to the output quality of a resulting MT system. Our aim is to reduce the number of partial translations in our training set and extract from them better mutual translations. Thus, we decide to set our threshold even higher, to 0.75. Furthermore, we proceed to find the one best segment pair created from each sentence pair, and only include that in our training set. Sometimes it comprises the whole sentence on both sides and sometimes only a part of either one or both the sentences. For almost half the sentence pairs all segment pair candidates are discarded as shown in Table 2. Using this approach, we produce $1.8M$ pairs, of which $1.2M$ were complete sentence pairs and over $600K$ containing partial sentences on either one or both sides. We add these to our foundation training set of $2M$ sentence pairs and then use this combined data to train a new translation model to investigate whether this processing approach affects the quality of translations, as measured by BLEU.

[5] http://commoncrawl.org/

Direction	BLEU	time
en→bn	**19.7**	10h52m
bn→en	26.8	10h32m

Table 3: BLEU scores for the final English–Bengali models, 2M pairs+fragments, which contain a total of 3.84M sentence pairs. Scores in bold are the highest for that translation direction.

4.3 Results

In order to evaluate if our methodology works to increase translation quality of an NMT system, we train new models using the same hyperparameters as before and evaluate them in terms of BLEU score, on the same test set as before. Table 3 shows how using our method gives us the highest BLEU score for en→bn, which is the translation direction we used to decide what data we should process for sub-sentence selection. This indicates that the added segment pairs add more value than if the same number of unchanged sentence pairs would have been added to the training data. By processing the dataset using our methodology, we reduce the training time by 65% while raising the BLEU score by 1.6. A statistical significance test performed by using MultEval (Clark et al., 2011) to do bootstrap resampling shows that our improved system, trained on less data, is significantly better than the baseline, with $p < 0.01$. It is also noteworthy that our system is only 0.6 BLEU below that of IndicTrans, reported in Section 4.1, which is almost seven times larger in terms of parameters and trained on the whole Samanantar dataset. We also tested for statistical significance between our system and IndicTrans and found that there is no statistically significant difference between the systems with $p > 0.01$. While we achieve the highest score for this translation direction using our refinement approach, the score is only slightly higher, 0.2 BLEU, than the highest score for selected subsets of the Samanantar corpus, the $3M$ sentence pair selection, and the difference is not statistically significant.

The highest scoring dataset for bn→en, significantly higher than the one created using our refinement approach, is the one containing $5M$ sentence pairs for training. That indicates that selecting data using different thresholds (see Section 4.2) for different translation directions could be beneficial before training a new MT model on the Samanantar corpus.

5 Data discarded during the Compilation of an English–Icelandic Parallel Corpus

We process the discarded English–Icelandic data in a slightly different manner. In our English–Bengali experiment we only considered subsentences within previously aligned pairs, and compared all the different concatenations of English chunks to the different combinations of Bengali chunks to find if we could raise the semantic score for the pair by removing parts from either or both sentences. For English–Icelandic, we instead consider our discarded sentences to be a comparable corpus and mine for sentence pairs from the pool of all segments in both languages. We use the approach of Steingrímsson et al. (2021b) using CLIR to create a candidate list and a logistic regression classifier to select the best sentence pairs from the list.

We start by deduplicating the discarded sentences and removing sentences that have less than three tokens that only contain alphabetical characters. This lowers the number of sentences we have to work with to $234,835$ English sentences and $242,456$ Icelandic sentences, as shown in Table 4. Next, we split all sentences into segments as we did with the English–Bengali data. As before, for splitting we use conjunctions, 'and' and 'or' for English and 'og' and 'eða' for Icelandic, as well as punctuation, the same symbols for both languages: .,;:?!()-"'|. We combine the segments into larger sentence parts and create all possible combinations of adjoining segments, ranging from single segments and up to recreating the original sentence, provided the

	English	Icelandic
Without alignments	$482,975$	$563,381$
Discarded in filtering	$350,964$	$364,267$
1. Total discarded	$833,939$	$927,648$
2. Min. three words + Deduplication	$234,835$	$242,456$
3. After sentence splits	$2,793,254$	$2,279,111$

Table 4: Number of discarded sentences used in the experiment and the resulting number of sentence segments, which are candidates for new alignments. The sentences are from the EEA subcorpus of ParIce, as described in Section 3.1.

combinations has a minimum length of three words, maximum length of 120 words, and that 70% of the tokens only contains alphabetical letters. This result in $2,793,254$ unique Icelandic sentences and sentence parts and $2,279,111$ English ones.

5.1 Mining for segment pairs

We start by extracting parallel sentence candidates using an inverted index-based CLIR tool called FaDA (Lohar et al., 2016), which can be applied to documents in any two languages, provided a bilingual dictionary is available. We use a publicly available English–Icelandic/Icelandic–English lexicon of $233K$ pairs (Steingrímsson et al., 2021). FaDA generates a list of 10 most likely candidates for each Icelandic and English sentence. We take an intersection of the two generated sets, resulting in $2,777,429$ pairs to be inspected further. For this result, we apply the following steps:

- We remove all segment pairs with major overlap, in which more than 60% of the tokens in either language are also present in the other.
- We calculate LaBSE score for all pairs. A manual inspection of higher scoring pairs for this language pair, indicates that there may be occasional valid pairs with scores as low as 0.3, so we use that as a cutoff point.
- If two sentence pairs are identical, apart from symbols and numbers, we select the one having the higher LaBSE score.
- We calculate LASER (Schwenk, 2018), NMTScore (Vamvas and Sennrich, 2022) and WAScore for the sentences and classify them using a logistic regression classifier trained on the training set introduced in Steingrímsson et al. (2021b). We discard all pairs rejected by the classifier.

Processing Step	No. Pairs left
FaDA	$2,777,429$
Acceptable Overlap	$1,878,202$
LaBSE minimum	$542,344$
Remove identical	$542,240$
Logistic regression filter	$342,066$
Multiple translations removed	$91,249$
Subsentence removal	$55,371$
Language filter	$36,200$

Table 5: English–Icelandic sentence pairs remaining after each step of processing pairs mined from the discarded data.

Dataset	en→is BLEU	is→en BLEU
903,692 pairs (-discarded data)	43.4	54.0
939,892 pairs (+discarded data)	***43.9***	**54.3**

Table 6: Best BLEU scores for models trained with and without the sentence paired mined from discarded data. Scores in bold are the highest scores and scores in bold and italic are significantly higher than other scores.

- We check if there is more than one pair containing each English or Icelandic sentence. If so, only the highest-scoring pair in terms of LaBSE is selected.
- For each sentence pair A, we check for other sentence pairs where the sentences are subsentences of A, such that the subsentence is between 67% and 100% of the length of the original one. If we find another sentence pair, B, having an Icelandic sentence B_{is} that is a substring of A_{is} and an English sentence B_{en} which is a substring of A_{en}, we select the pair that has a higher LaBSE score and discard the other one. This way, we remove nearly identical sentence pairs originating from the same sentences.
- Finally, we run our pairs through a *fasttext* (Joulin et al., 2017) language filter, accepting pairs if the language of each sentences is correctly predicted in the top two predictions of the filter. We selected the top two predictions as we noticed that for Icelandic sentences, Icelandic was often not the first prediction, but most often in the top two predictions, unless they were somehow defective.

Table 5 shows the number of sentence pairs remaining after each processing step. After the final step, $36,200$ sentence pairs remain, mined from the $234,835$ English sentences and $242,456$ Icelandic sentences that had been previously discarded. We add these pairs to the training data previously acquired by sentence alignment and filtering, resulting in a total of $939,892$ sentence pairs. We train Transformer$_{BASE}$ models and evaluate on an in-domain evaluation set as detailed in Section 3.2. We compare the results to systems trained without the supplemental sentence pairs mined from discarded data. The systems trained with the segment pairs mined from the discarded data have slightly higher BLEU scores, but only en→is scores significantly higher than the system trained without the supplemental segment pairs. Results are given in Table 6.

6 Conclusions and Future Work

In this paper, we set out to answer whether deficient sentence pairs in a parallel corpus could be identified and refined and whether data commonly discarded when compiling parallel corpora or training NMT systems could be mined for parallel sentence pairs, that are still beneficial for training. We conducted two experiments to answer these questions. First, we tried re-evaluating sentence pairs in an English–Bengali parallel corpus in an attempt to remove extraneous data from partially parallel pairs. By partially parallel pairs we mean that a part of either sentence can align perfectly with either the whole or a part of the other sentence. Second, we collected all sentences discarded when an English–Icelandic parallel corpus was compiled, segmented them to create multiple sub-sentential variants, and treated as comparable corpora for mining parallel pairs

By using our approaches, the quality of our training corpus improved, leading to significantly better quality MT models, as measured by BLEU, when translating from English and into either Bengali or Icelandic. However, when translating into English we did not see this effect as clearly. In the English–Bengali experiment the data selection aimed at increasing English→Bengali translation, which may explain the effect we see there, and for English→Icelandic the score rose slightly, but not significantly when the sentence pairs mined from discarded data was added. In that case the low improvement is most likely explained be the small size of the additional data, which only increased the size of the training data by 4%.

In future work we want to experiment with other methods of segmenting sentences, such as by using constituency parsing. The approach we used in this paper for segmenting was simple and easy to implement. More sophisticated segmentation may allow for more precise recombinations of sentence parts, for example by skipping parenthetical clauses or other insertions which may not be represented in both sentences. We also want to investigate whether our approaches also show positive results for other language pairs

Our experiments indicate that there is a potential in taking a second look at data that would usually be discarded, as well as in refining partially aligned sentence pairs. We showed that parallel sub-sentences are useful to acquire translation knowledge and extracting them can lead to significant improvement in performance, even using simple approaches. The methodology can thus have an impact on training future MT systems.

Finally, the training time for the different models, shown in Tables 1 and 3, indicates that smaller and more accurate training corpora have the added benefit of helping with faster convergence. In our case, training time is reduced by 65% from using the whole dataset to using our selected subset for training en→bn. The model also comes close to reaching the quality of the much larger IndicTrans model. This can translate into less need for storage and less resources at training and inference time, which is in line with a call to greener and more sustainable models of AI which consume less electricity, output fewer emissions, and perform on the whole as well as larger models, see e.g. Yusuf et al. (2021) and Jooste et al. (2022).

Acknowledgements

This work was supported by the Icelandic Centre for Research (RANNIS), grant number 228654-051, and by the ADAPT Centre for Digital Content Technology which is funded under the Science Foundation Ireland (SFI) Research Centres Programme (Grant No. 13/RC/2106) and is co-funded under the European Regional Development Fund.

References

Akhbardeh, F., Arkhangorodsky, A., Biesialska, M., Bojar, O., Chatterjee, R., Chaudhary, V., Costa-jussa, M. R., España-Bonet, C., Fan, A., Federmann, C., Freitag, M., Graham, Y., Grundkiewicz, R., Haddow, B., Harter, L., Heafield, K., Homan, C., Huck, M., Amponsah-Kaakyire, K., Kasai, J., Khashabi, D., Knight, K., Kocmi, T., Koehn, P., Lourie, N., Monz, C., Morishita, M., Nagata, M., Nagesh, A., Nakazawa, T., Negri, M., Pal, S., Tapo, A. A., Turchi, M., Vydrin, V., and Zampieri, M. (2021). Findings of the 2021 Conference on Machine Translation (WMT21). In *Proceedings of the Sixth Conference on Machine Translation*, pages 1–88, Online.

Artetxe, M. and Schwenk, H. (2019). Massively Multilingual Sentence Embeddings for Zero-Shot Cross-Lingual Transfer and Beyond. *Trans. Assoc. Comput. Linguistics*, 7:597–610.

Bal, S., Mahanta, S., Mandal, L., and Parekh, R. (2019). Bilingual Machine Translation: English to Bengali. In Chakraborty, M., Chakrabarti, S., Balas, V. E., and Mandal, J. K., editors, *Proceedings of International Ethical Hacking Conference 2018*, pages 247–259, Singapore.

Barkarson, S. and Steingrímsson, S. (2019). Compiling and Filtering ParIce: An English-

Icelandic Parallel Corpus. In *Proceedings of the 22nd Nordic Conference on Computational Linguistics*, Turku, Finland.

Barkarson, S., Steingrímsson, S., Ingimundarson, F. Á., Hafsteinsdóttir, H., and Magnússon, Á. D. (2021). ParIce dev/test sets 21.10. CLARIN-IS.

Brandt, M. D., Loftsson, H., Sigurþórsson, H., and Tyers, F. M. (2011). Apertium-IceNLP: A rule-based Icelandic to English machine translation system. In *Proceedings of the 15th Annual conference of the European Association for Machine Translation*, Leuven, Belgium.

Clark, J. H., Dyer, C., Lavie, A., and Smith, N. A. (2011). Better Hypothesis Testing for Statistical Machine Translation: Controlling for Optimizer Instability. In *Proceedings of the 49th Annual Meeting of the Association for Computational Linguistics: Human Language Technologies*, pages 176–181, Portland, Oregon, USA.

Feng, F., Yang, Y., Cer, D., Arivazhagan, N., and Wang, W. (2022). Language-agnostic BERT Sentence Embedding. In *Proceedings of the 60th Annual Meeting of the Association for Computational Linguistics (Volume 1: Long Papers)*, pages 878–891, Dublin, Ireland.

Forcada, M., Ginestí-Rosell, M., Nordfalk, J., O'Regan, J., Ortiz-Rojas, S., Pérez-Ortiz, J., Sánchez-Martínez, F., Ramírez-Sánchez, G., and Tyers, F. (2011). Apertium: A free/open-source platform for rule-based machine translation. *Machine Translation*, 25:127–144.

Goyal, N., Gao, C., Chaudhary, V., Chen, P.-J., Wenzek, G., Ju, D., Krishnan, S., Ranzato, M., Guzmán, F., and Fan, A. (2022). The Flores-101 Evaluation Benchmark for Low-Resource and Multilingual Machine Translation. *Transactions of the Association for Computational Linguistics*, 10:522–538.

Hangya, V. and Fraser, A. (2019). Unsupervised Parallel Sentence Extraction with Parallel Segment Detection Helps Machine Translation. In *Proceedings of the 57th Annual Meeting of the Association for Computational Linguistics*, pages 1224–1234, Florence, Italy.

Jónsson, H. P., Símonarson, H. B., Snæbjarnarson, V., Steingrímsson, S., and Loftsson, H. (2020). Experimenting with Different Machine Translation Models in Medium-Resource Settings. In Sojka, P., Kopecek, I., Pala, K., and Horák, A., editors, *Text, Speech, and Dialogue - 23rd International Conference, TSD 2020, Brno, Czech Republic, September 8-11, 2020, Proceedings*, volume 12284 of *Lecture Notes in Computer Science*, pages 95–103.

Jooste, W., Haque, R., and Way, A. (2022). Knowledge Distillation: A Method for Making Neural Machine Translation More Efficient. *Information*, 13(2).

Joulin, A., Grave, E., Bojanowski, P., and Mikolov, T. (2017). Bag of Tricks for Efficient Text Classification. In *Proceedings of the 15th Conference of the European Chapter of the Association for Computational Linguistics: Volume 2, Short Papers*, pages 427–431, Valencia, Spain.

Karimi, A., Ansari, E., and Sadeghi Bigham, B. (2018). Extracting an English-Persian Parallel Corpus from Comparable Corpora. In *Proceedings of the Eleventh International Conference on Language Resources and Evaluation (LREC 2018)*, pages 3477–3482, Miyazaki, Japan.

Koehn, P., Khayrallah, H., Heafield, K., and Forcada, M. L. (2018). Findings of the WMT 2018 Shared Task on Parallel Corpus Filtering. In *Proceedings of the Third Conference on Machine Translation: Shared Task Papers*, pages 726–739, Belgium, Brussels. Association for Computational Linguistics.

Lohar, P., Ganguly, D., Afli, H., Way, A., and Jones, G. J. F. (2016). FaDA: Fast Document Aligner using Word Embedding. *The Prague Bulletin of Mathematical Linguistics*, 106:169–179.

Munteanu, D. S. and Marcu, D. (2006). Extracting Parallel Sub-Sentential Fragments from Non-Parallel Corpora. In *Proceedings of the 21st International Conference on Computational Linguistics and 44th Annual Meeting of the Association for Computational Linguistics*, pages 81–88, Sydney, Australia.

Ott, M., Edunov, S., Baevski, A., Fan, A., Gross, S., Ng, N., Grangier, D., and Auli, M. (2019). fairseq: A Fast, Extensible Toolkit for Sequence Modeling. In *Proceedings of the 2019 Conference of the North American Chapter of the Association for Computational Linguistics (Demonstrations)*, pages 48–53, Minneapolis, Minnesota.

Papineni, K., Roukos, S., Ward, T., and Zhu, W.-J. (2002). BLEU: a Method for Automatic Evaluation of Machine Translation. In *Proceedings of the 40th Annual Meeting of the Association for Computational Linguistics*, pages 311–318, Philadelphia, Pennsylvania, USA.

Paul, S. and Purkhyastha, B. S. (2020). English to Bengali Neural Machine Translation System for the Aviation Domain. *INFOCOMP Journal of Computer Science*, 19(2):78–97.

Post, M. (2018). A Call for Clarity in Reporting BLEU Scores. In *Proceedings of the Third Conference on Machine Translation: Research Papers*, pages 186–191, Belgium, Brussels.

Ramesh, G., Doddapaneni, S., Bheemaraj, A., Jobanputra, M., AK, R., Sharma, A., Sahoo, S., Diddee, H., J, M., Kakwani, D., Kumar, N., Pradeep, A., Nagaraj, S., Deepak, K., Raghavan, V., Kunchukuttan, A., Kumar, P., and Khapra, M. S. (2022). Samanantar: The Largest Publicly Available Parallel Corpora Collection for 11 Indic Languages. *Transactions of the Association for Computational Linguistics*, 10:145–162.

Schwenk, H. (2018). Filtering and Mining Parallel Data in a Joint Multilingual Space. In *Proceedings of the 56th Annual Meeting of the Association for Computational Linguistics (Volume 2: Short Papers)*, pages 228–234, Melbourne, Australia.

Sennrich, R., Haddow, B., and Birch, A. (2016). Neural Machine Translation of Rare Words with Subword Units. In *Proceedings of the 54th Annual Meeting of the Association for Computational Linguistics*, pages 1715–1725, Berlin, Germany.

Sennrich, R. and Zhang, B. (2019). Revisiting Low-Resource Neural Machine Translation: A Case Study. In *Proceedings of the 57th Annual Meeting of the Association for Computational Linguistics*, pages 211–221, Florence, Italy.

Siddique, S., , Ahmed, T., Talukder, M. R. A., and Uddin, M. M. (2020). English to Bangla Machine Translation Using Recurrent Neural Network. *International Journal of Future Computer and Communication*, pages 46–51.

Steingrímsson, S., Loftsson, H., and Way, A. (2021a). CombAlign: a tool for obtaining high-quality word alignments. In *Proceedings of the 23rd Nordic Conference on Computational Linguistics (NoDaLiDa)*, pages 64–73, Reykjavik, Iceland (Online).

Steingrímsson, S., Loftsson, H., and Way, A. (2023). Filtering matters: Experiments in filtering training sets for machine translation. In *Proceedings of the 24th Nordic Conference on Computational Linguistics (NoDaLiDa)*, pages 588–600, Tórshavn, Faroe Islands.

Steingrímsson, S., Lohar, P., Loftsson, H., and Way, A. (2021b). Effective Bitext Extraction From Comparable Corpora Using a Combination of Three Different Approaches. In *Proceedings of the 14th Workshop on Building and Using Comparable Corpora (BUCC 2021)*, pages 8–17, Online (Virtual Mode).

Steingrímsson, S., Obrien, L. J., Ingimundarson, F. Á., Magnússon, Á. D., Andrésdóttir, Þ. D., and Eiríksdóttir, I. G. (2021). English-Icelandic/Icelandic-English glossary 21.09. CLARIN-IS.

Vamvas, J. and Sennrich, R. (2022). NMTScore: A multilingual analysis of translation-based text similarity measures. In *Findings of the Association for Computational Linguistics: EMNLP 2022*, pages 198–213, Abu Dhabi, United Arab Emirates.

Vaswani, A., Shazeer, N., Parmar, N., Uszkoreit, J., Jones, L., Gomez, A. N., Kaiser, Ł., and Polosukhin, I. (2017). Attention Is All You Need. In Guyon, I., Luxburg, U. V., Bengio, S., Wallach, H., Fergus, R., Vishwanathan, S., and Garnett, R., editors, *Advances in Neural Information Processing Systems*, volume 30.

Yusuf, M., Surana, P., Gupta, G., and Ramesh, K. (2021). Curb Your Carbon Emissions: Benchmarking Carbon Emissions in Machine Translation. *ArXiv*, abs/2109.12584.

Development of Urdu-English Religious Domain Parallel Corpus

Noor e Hira noorehira94@gmail.com
Department of Computer Science, Fatima Jinnah Women University, Pakistan
Sadaf Abdul Rauf sadaf.abdulrauf@gmail.com
Department of Computer Science, Fatima Jinnah Women University, Pakistan

Abstract

Despite the abundance of monolingual corpora accessible online, there remains a scarcity of domain specific parallel corpora. This scarcity poses a challenge in the development of robust translation systems tailored for such specialized domains. Addressing this gap, we have developed a parallel religious domain corpus for Urdu-English. This corpus consists of 18,426 parallel sentences from Sunan Dawood, carefully curated to capture the unique linguistic and contextual aspects of religious texts. The developed corpus is then used to train Urdu-English religious domain Neural Machine Translation (NMT) systems, the best system scored 27.9 BLEU points.

1 Introduction

Neural Machine Translation Bahdanau et al. (2014) has been a field of intense attention for researchers since its advent. It has shown explosive increase in research, introducing new paradigms, revealing new approaches, achieving new milestones and ultimately gaining far better accuracy levels than the previous statistical machine translation (SMT) approaches. NMT Research is not only focused on improving the translation quality of high-resource language pairs, but it also investigates techniques to train machines under different scenarios including monolingual Gibadullin et al. (2019), low-resource Ranathunga et al. (2023), multilingual Dabre et al. (2020), document level NMT Maruf et al. (2021), and much more.

These investigations open new hopes for NMT, but the availability of parallel corpus for training NMT systems is the bottle neck factor to improve translation quality. The more this factor is important the more it is difficult to obtain Munteanu and Marcu (2005); Abdul-Rauf and Schwenk (2009). After years of research on MT till today, only a few languages have huge parallel corpora available, some others have moderate parallel corpus whereas many languages still lack the availability of any parallel corpus for their training.

Training standard NMT systems is a real challenge in low resource settings. Scarcity of available parallel corpus for low resource languages affect translation quality of NMT systems. Same is the case for training domain specific NMT systems, which is subject to the availability of domain specific parallel corpus. Hence, there is a need to investigate and analyse different NMT techniques for low resource settings including domain specific NMT training and adopt the possible ways to improve Urdu-English machine translation which falls under the category of low resource language.

Development of parallel corpus for languages is a time-consuming and tedious task, which

Proceedings of the Second Workshop on Corpus Generation and Corpus Augmentation for Machine Translation, pages 14–21
September 5, 2023, Macau SAR, China.

sometimes requires the input of native speakers as well Callison-Burch et al. (2011). The Urdu-English parallel corpora as investigated by Abdul Rauf et al. (2020) are not available in abundance. David M. et al. (2021) provided statistics about Urdu highlighting the need of parallel corpora.

The availability of massive monolingual religious translations in English and Urdu motivated our research to develop a religious domain Urdu-English parallel corpus. Despite the abundant availability of religious corpora in multiple languages, parallel corpora are still limited. To our knowledge, $UMC005$ is the only religious domain parallel Urdu-English corpus publicly available (Jawaid and Zeman, 2011; Abdul Rauf et al., 2020). The creation of such corpora for Urdu, a low-resource language holds immense significance, as it enables the adaptation of machine translation systems tailored to this specialized domain.

We have developed a bilingual Urdu-English religious corpus of 18,426 sentences [1]. Section 3 of this paper outlines the detailed steps and procedures taken for the development of this religious parallel corpus. We have also trained NMT models specialized for this domain where the best BLUE score is 27.9. Our NMT experiments are described in Section 4.

2 Related Work

We report the works related to publicly available religious domain parallel corpora specifically the hadith corpora. Altammami et al. (2020) publish the first publicly available bilingual parallel corpus of Islamic Hadith extracted from the six canonical Hadith books; using a domain-specific tool for Hadith segmentation, resulting in bilingual English-Arabic parallel corpus[2] of 39,038 annotated Hadiths. However, Sunan Dawood is automatically aligned in their work where they report an accuracy of 92%, whereas our corpus is aligned and checked manually. Abdul Rauf et al. (2020) provide details about all the publicly available corpora for Urdu-English language pair in biomedical, religious, technological, and general domain. We have used all the corpora mentioned in the study for our NMT experiments.

3 Methodology

Despite the fact that religious books and documents are available over the internet in massive amounts, along with their translations in many languages including English and Urdu, the creation of a religious domain Urdu-English parallel corpus is not easy as both languages have far different sentence segmentation and arrangement. The text of the available translations is coherent, as per the needs of language proficiency and flow. The difference in sentence structure of both the languages and the coherency of the text makes automatic sentence segmentation almost impossible. Our corpus development cycle includes four different stages, collection of available translations, manual filtering of collected data, extraction of parallel translations, and sentence-level segmentation of parallel texts.

3.1 Source Data Collection

The first step of our corpus development cycle included the search and collection of available translations of religious texts. Although, abundant religious text is available over the internet for English Urdu language pair, but the format of the documents is not suitable for MT corpus development research. The foremost hurdle faced during corpus collection was to search for books or documents in Unicode format. We were able to find and download *Sunan Abu Dawood*, a hadith book among the six major hadith books collected by Abu Dawud al-Sijistani from

[1] `https://github.com/sabdul111/SunanDaud-Urdu-English-Parallel-Corpus`

[2] The corpus is named as *Leeds and King Saud University (LK) Hadith corpus*

Figure 1: Sample of Sunan Abu Dawood files after extraction from PDF.

$IslamicUrduBooks$ [3]. The website provides access to many hadith books in unicode format, but only *Sunan Abu Dawood* was available with English and Urdu translations. Arabic text of each hadith is followed by its Urdu and English translation respectively. Few hadiths had some extra information embedded in between Urdu and English translations of Arabic text. Figure 1 shows the format of Sunan Abu Dawood file.

[3]https://islamicurdubooks.com/books/word-files/

Source	Files	Words		lines
		English	Urdu	
SD1	3,194	83,093	99,770	8,160
SD2	2,952	80,775	96,784	8,495
SD3	1,878	19,639	25,594	1,771
Total	8,024	183,507	222,148	18,426

Table 1: Urdu-English Religious Domain Corpus, `SD1` represents Sunan Abu Dawood volume 1, `SD2` volume 2, and `SD3` volume 3

3.2 Data Filtering

We manually inspected the files and applied different filtering steps to convert them to parallel bi-texts. Document filtration included removal of content tables, figures, and objects. The text file was then manually inspected to identify the extra information embedded in between the translations. Such information had specific keywords such as `Takhreej Darul Da'wah`, `Wazahat` etc. Scripts were used where appropriate to remove extra content using specified keywords. Additionally, hadith numbers and blank lines were eliminated.

3.3 Parallel Translation Extraction

In this step, the filtered files were further examined to ensure that each hadith contained translations in both English and Urdu languages. The line numbers of the English text were observed, as each hadith consisted of Arabic text on the first line, Urdu text on the second line, and English text on the third line. Any discrepancies in the line numbers were manually corrected by backtracking through the file to identify and remove the problematic content. In cases where translations were missing in one language, a placeholder text such as "translation not available" was added in the respective language to maintain line number consistency without compromising the contents for the other two languages. Scripts were utilized to separate the text of each hadith into three distinct files: one for Arabic, one for Urdu, and one for English. A manual inspection of the main file was conducted to verify the accurate extraction of each language's text. If successful, the process moved forward; otherwise, steps were retraced and adjustments were made to address any errors.

3.4 Parallel Sentence Splitting

This step involved splitting the extracted text into parallel smaller phrases or sentences, focusing on the English and Urdu files. Manual splitting was chosen over automatic methods to ensure corpus content accuracy. Volunteers with proficiency in these languages were chosen from graduate students. To assess the volunteers' understanding, an initial submission of a few hadiths was evaluated. Only a small percentage demonstrated complete comprehension, prompting adjustments, and the provision of a demo video. Subsequent submissions showed significant improvement, reinforcing the chosen approach. Each student's work was reviewed to ensure correct alignment, and files with errors were reassigned to students with greater accuracy.

First two volumes of Sunan Abu Dawood, along with selected hadiths from the third volume, were successfully processed. Table 1 presents the statistics for the developed religious corpus, with `SD1` representing Sunan Abu Dawood Volume 1, `SD2` denoting Volume 2, and `SD3` referring to Volume 3.

4 Urdu-English Neural Machine Translation

This section describes the results of NMT systems trained using our developed corpus and other publicly available Urdu-English corpora.

4.1 Corpora

The study of Abdul Rauf et al. (2020) provides details about all the publicly available corpora for Urdu-English language pair. We have used all the corpora mentioned in the study and some additional corpora as explained below and listed in Table 2.

- The Emille[4] (Baker et al., 2002) is a 97 million word corpus developed under a joint project of Lancaster University, UK, and the Central Institute of Indian Languages (CIIL), Mysore, India. It is a collection of monolingual, parallel and annotated corpora for fourteen South Asian Languages including Assamese, Bengali, Gujarati, Hindi, Kannada, Kashmiri, Malayalam, Marathi, Oriya, Punjabi, Sinhala, Tamil, Telegu and Urdu. The corpus comprises of data in both textual and spoken formats and is freely distributed by ELRA (European Language Resource Association) for research purposes.

- Indic[5] is a corpus comprising texts for six indian languages including Bengali, Hindi, Malayalam, Tamil, Telugu and Urdu. The corpus was developed from top 100 most visited documents of Wikipedia. Corpus was constructed using Amazon's Mechanical Turk (MTurk) for crowd sourcing. (Post et al., 2012).

- OPUS[6] (Tiedemann, 2012) is a resource which provides access to freely available annotated parallel corpora, collected from web resources and processed automatically. OPUS contains fourteen different corpora for Urdu-English language pair, including CCAligned, CCMatrix, GlobalVoices, GNOME, Mozilla, OpenSubtitles, QED, Tanzil, Tatoeba, TED, Tico, Ubuntu, Wikimedia and XLEnt. We used all these corpora for our experiments.

- Jawaid and Zeman (2011) collected translations of Quran and Bible from web, which is different from Tanzil corpus provided by OPUS. Their collection, UMC005[7], contains two other corpora for Urdu-English language pair, but Only Quran and Bible are available for free.

- Urdu translations of Wall Street Journal (WSJ), a subset of *Penn Treebank* Marcus et al. (1993) have been released by CLE[8]. We collected the Urdu translations of this corpus form official website of CLE and their corresponding English translations were awarded from LDC as data scholarship we applied for.

- QBJ (Quran+Bible+Joshua) corpus is another collection of freely available Urdu-English corpus. It has 1.02M English words and 1.13M Urdu words.

- PMindia is a parallel corpus of Indian languages extracted from the website of the Prime Minister of India (www.pmindia.gov.in). The corpus provides parallel sentences for thirteen major languages of India.

- SD is the Urdu-English religious domain corpus having parallel ahadith from 3 volumes of Sunan Abu Dawood that we developed during this work.

[4]The Emille/CIIL Corpus:ID:ELRA-W0037
[5]http://joshua-decoder.org/indian-parallel-corpora/
[6]http://opus.nlpl.eu/
[7]https://ufal.mff.cuni.cz/umc/005-en-ur/
[8]http://www.cle.org.pk/

Category	Corpus	tokens		Sentences
		English	Urdu	
Out-domain	CCAligned	18M	23M	1,371,930
	CCMatrix	67M	80M	6,094,149
	Emily	89K	0.1M	5,877
	Global Voices	72K	82K	4,103
	Gnome	42K	50,k	11,535
	Indic	0.5M	0.6M	35,139
	Open-Subtitles	0.17M	2.0M	29,074
	PMindia	0.2M	0.26M	11,167
	QED	0.25M	0.29M	19,053
	Tatoeba	10K	12k	1,667
	TED	0.26	0.32	15,755
	Tico	70K	91K	3,071
	Treebank	0.13M	0.18	5,693
	Ubuntu	10K	12K	3,025
	Wikimedia	2.0M	3M	43,168
	XLEnt	2.0M	2.1M	746,804
	Total	**91.5M**	**111M**	**8.4M**
In-domain	Tanzil	19M	23M	748320
	OBJ	1.0M	1.1M	49510
	Bible	0.21M	0.20M	7957
	Quran	0.25M	0.24M	6414
	SunanDawood	0.19M	0.23M	20678
	Total	**20.1M**	**24.8M**	**832879**

Table 2: Indomain and out domain Urdu-English training corpora

ID	Train Set (No of sentences)	Size	scores
M1	Out_D	8,401,210	14.5
M2	In_D	832,879	**27.9**
M3	$Out_D \xrightarrow{adapt} In_D$	832,879	21.4

Table 3: BLEU scores

4.2 Preprocessing

Corpus preprocessing is an essential part of building machine learning systems. Three of the corpora, Emillie, NLT and Penn Tree-bank were partially aligned. We used LF sentence aligner[9] to align these corpora but due to the topological differences between the two languages results obtained from LF aligner were not accurate and, thus manual alignment was done to ensure correctness. Tokenization, using mosses tokenizer[10], truecasing and BPE (Sennrich et al., 2016), were applied to all the corpora during pre-processing.

[9] https://sourceforge.net/projects/aligner/

[10] `https://github.com/moses-smt/mosesdecoder/blob/master/scripts/tokenizer/tokenizer.perl`

4.3 NMT Experiments

We trained three NMT models using the transformer (Vaswani et al., 2017) architecture. The models were evaluated using religious domain test set as our objective was to build and improve the accuracy of religious domain translation models. The religious domain Urdu-English corpora was split in a ratio of 8:1:1 for train, validation and test-set respectively.

The $M1$ model was trained using out-domain corpus, i.e. all the Urdu-English corpus other than the religious domain and it scored 14.5 BLEU points.

$M2$, the model trained on in-domain data outscored $M1$ by 13.4 BLEU points. This result is inline with existing research highlighting the importance of domain for the training corpora. A system built on the same domain as the test set will give better translations.

Lastly we experimented with domain adaptation $M3$, i.e. improve domain-specific machine translation using indomain data to adapt the out domain model towards the religious domain. For $M3$, though performance improved as compared to $M1$ giving 21.4 BLEU scores on the test-set but still it did not outperform $M2$.

Our results show the importance of in-domain corpus. System trained on only small amount of religious domain corpus is better than system trained on large general domain data and fine tuned on in domain corpora.

5 Conclusion

In this paper, we have successfully tackled the challenges of developing a parallel Urdu-English corpus in the religious domain. The meticulous process of acquiring, processing, and aligning the data resulted in a corpus comprising 18,426 lines. The developed corpus underwent a thorough analysis to ensure the accuracy and integrity of data. It is then used to train Urdu-English religious domain NMT systems, the best systems scored 27.9 BLEU points. These findings underscore the effectiveness of the corpus in enabling accurate and meaningful translations within the religious context.

Acknowledgments

This study is funded by the National Research Program for Universities (NRPU) by Higher Education Commission of Pakistan (5469/Punjab/NRPU/R&D/HEC/2016).

References

Abdul Rauf, S., Abida, S., Hira, N.-e., Zahra, S., Parvez, D., Bashir, J., and Majid, Q.-u.-a. (2020). On the exploration of English to Urdu machine translation. In *Proceedings of the 1st Joint Workshop on Spoken Language Technologies for Under-resourced languages (SLTU) and Collaboration and Computing for Under-Resourced Languages (CCURL)*, pages 285–293, Marseille, France. European Language Resources association.

Abdul-Rauf, S. and Schwenk, H. (2009). On the use of comparable corpora to improve SMT performance. In *Proceedings of the 12th Conference of the European Chapter of the ACL (EACL 2009)*, pages 16–23, Athens, Greece. Association for Computational Linguistics.

Altammami, S., Atwell, E., and Alsalka, A. (2020). The arabic-english parallel corpus of authentic hadith. *International Journal on Islamic Applications in Computer Science And Technology*, 8(2).

Bahdanau, D., Cho, K., and Bengio, Y. (2014). Neural machine translation by jointly learning to align and translate. *CoRR*, abs/1409.0473.

Baker, P., Hardie, A., McEnery, T., Cunningham, H., and Gaizauskas, R. J. (2002). Emille, a 67-million word corpus of indic languages: Data collection, mark-up and harmonisation. In *LREC*.

Callison-Burch, C., Koehn, P., Monz, C., and Zaidan, O. F. (2011). Findings of the 2011 workshop on statistical machine translation. In *Proceedings of the Sixth Workshop on Statistical Machine Translation*, pages 22–64. Association for Computational Linguistics.

Dabre, R., Chu, C., and Kunchukuttan, A. (2020). A survey of multilingual neural machine translation. *ACM Comput. Surv.*, 53(5).

David M., E., Simons, G. F., and Fennig, C. D. (2021). Ethnologue: Languages of the world. twenty-fourth edition. dallas, texas: Sil international.

Gibadullin, I., Valeev, A., Khusainova, A., and Khan, A. (2019). A survey of methods to leverage monolingual data in low-resource neural machine translation. *arXiv preprint arXiv:1910.00373*.

Jawaid, B. and Zeman, D. (2011). Word-order issues in english-to-urdu statistical machine translation. *Prague Bull. Math. Linguistics*, 95:87–106.

Marcus, M. P., Santorini, B., and Marcinkiewicz, M. A. (1993). Building a large annotated corpus of English: The Penn Treebank. *Computational Linguistics*, 19(2):313–330.

Maruf, S., Saleh, F., and Haffari, G. (2021). A survey on document-level neural machine translation: Methods and evaluation. *ACM Comput. Surv.*, 54(2).

Munteanu, D. S. and Marcu, D. (2005). Improving machine translation performance by exploiting non-parallel corpora. *Computational Linguistics*, 31(4):477–504.

Post, M., Callison-Burch, C., and Osborne, M. (2012). Constructing parallel corpora for six indian languages via crowdsourcing. *Wmt-2012*, pages 401–409.

Ranathunga, S., Lee, E.-S. A., Prifti Skenduli, M., Shekhar, R., Alam, M., and Kaur, R. (2023). Neural machine translation for low-resource languages: A survey. *ACM Comput. Surv.*, 55(11).

Sennrich, R., Haddow, B., and Birch, A. (2016). Neural machine translation of rare words with subword units. In *Proceedings of the 54th Annual Meeting of the Association for Computational Linguistics (Volume 1: Long Papers)*, pages 1715–1725, Berlin, Germany.

Tiedemann, J. (2012). Parallel Data, Tools and Interfaces in OPUS. In Nicoletta Calzolari (Conference Chair) and Khalid Choukri and Thierry Declerck and Mehmet Ugur Dogan and Bente Maegaard and Joseph Mariani and Jan Odijk and Stelios Piperidis, editor, *Proceedings of the Eight International Conference on Language Resources and Evaluation (LREC'12)*. European Language Resources Association (ELRA), Istanbul, Turkey.

Vaswani, A., Shazeer, N., Parmar, N., Uszkoreit, J., Jones, L., Gomez, A. N., Kaiser, L. u., and Polosukhin, I. (2017). Attention is all you need. In Guyon, I., Luxburg, U. V., Bengio, S., Wallach, H., Fergus, R., Vishwanathan, S., and Garnett, R., editors, *Advances in Neural Information Processing Systems 30*, pages 5998–6008. Curran Associates, Inc.

Findings of the CoCo4MT 2023 Shared Task on Corpus Construction for Machine Translation

Organizers
Ananya Ganesh[1] ananya.ganesh@colorado.edu
Marine Carpuat[2] marine@umd.edu
William Chen[3] williamchen@cmu.edu
Katharina Kann[1] katharina.kann@colorado.edu
Constantine Lignos[4] lignos@brandeis.edu
John E. Ortega[5] j.ortega@northeastern.edu
Jonne Saleva[4] jonnesaleva@brandeis.edu
Shabnam Tafreshi[2] stafresh@umd.edu
Rodolfo Zevallos[6] rodolfojoel.zevallos@upf.edu

[1]University of Colorado Boulder
[2]University of Maryland
[3]Carnegie Mellon University
[4]Brandeis University
[5]Northeastern University
[6]Universitat Pompeu Fabra

Abstract

This paper provides an overview of the first shared task on choosing beneficial instances for machine translation, conducted as part of the CoCo4MT 2023 Workshop at MTSummit. This shared task was motivated by the need to make the data annotation process for machine translation more efficient, particularly for low-resource languages for which collecting human translations may be difficult or expensive. The task involved developing methods for selecting the most beneficial instances for training a machine translation system without access to an existing parallel dataset in the target language, such that the best selected instances can then be manually translated. Two teams participated in the shared task, namely the `Williams` team and the `AST` team. Submissions were evaluated by training a machine translation model on each submission's chosen instances, and comparing their performance with the chRF++ score. The system that ranked first is by the `Williams` team, that finds representative instances by clustering the training data.

1 Introduction

It is a well-known fact that machine translation (MT) systems, especially those that use deep learning, require massive amounts of data. Some of the types of resources available are monolingual, multilingual, translation memories, and lexicons. Those types of resources are gener-

Proceedings of the Second Workshop on Corpus Generation and Corpus Augmentation for Machine Translation, pages 22–27
September 5, 2023, Macau SAR, China.

ally created for formal purposes such as parliamentary proceedings (Koehn, 2005), particularly when the data is parallel. The quality and abundance of such resources for niche or rare domains such as medicine or science is limited, meaning that focused annotation efforts are required when an MT system for such domains needs to be developed. Additionally, corpora for low-resource languages, languages with less digital resources available, tends to be less abundant and of lower quality.

While MT systems developed using unsupervised methods and monolingual corpora have been effective to a great extent (Lample et al., 2018; Liu et al., 2020), parallel data is still crucial, particularly in the case of low-resource languages, as shown by Kim et al. (2020). However, collection or annotation of parallel data is constrained by access to bilingual translators, who may be rare or highly expensive. Therefore, making the data annotation process cost effective by ensuring that the translated instances are of high quality and will lead to high-performing MT systems when used for training. For maximum value, it is desirable to have access to this information *before* a dataset in the target language is actually constructed. That is, if the annotation budget only permits a limited number of sentences to be translated, but there is a large number of source language sentences, it is optimal to choose sentences for human translation that are expected to be highly beneficial.

Towards making the annotation process more efficient, in this shared task, we solicit methods for the identification of such beneficial instances effectively without requiring training data in the target language [1]. We provide multi-way parallel data from several high-resource languages such as English and German, which can be used to identify instances that are helpful for model training, such as by observing training dynamics (Bhatnagar et al., 2022). Participants are required to submit the English sentences corresponding to instances chosen by their algorithms as the most beneficial. Notably, this task does not necessarily require training MT models – simple heuristics that can indicate the quality of an instance can also be submitted. The performance of all submissions, including the baselines, are evaluated by training an MT model (specifically, mBART) on the selected instances. We use the chrF++ metric (Popović, 2017) to compare all systems.

The shared task officially began on May 19, 2023 with the release of all training data. Baselines were then added on June 6, 2023 [2]. Interested participants were asked to officially register for the shared task through a Google Forms submission, on which four teams registered. The participation phase concluded on July 21, 2023, until which date submissions could be made by sending text files with the chosen instances to the official CoCo4MT 2023 email address. Of the four teams that registered, only two teams made a submission before the conclusion of the shared task. Both teams described their methods and shared an open-source implementation through a system description paper.

2 Data

All data used for model training, evaluation and instance selection is sourced from the Johns Hopkins University Bible corpus (McCarthy et al., 2020). This is a multi-way parallel corpus containing verses from the Christian Bible translated into more than 1600 languages.

Languages: As outlined above, we provide data for a set of "high-resource" languages, which are intended to be used for developing systems to select beneficial instances. For this purpose, we choose the languages English, German, Indonesian, and Korean. We also provide data in

[1] Website describing the workshop and shared task is at `https://sites.google.com/view/coco4mt`

[2] Data, baselines and processing scripts can be found at `https://github.com/ananyaganesh/coco4mt-shared-task`

the "low-resource" languages of Gujarati, French and Burmese for participants to evaluate the performance of their methods. This setting can be considered to be a simulated low-resource setting, since for the purpose of this dataset, all languages are multi-way parallel. Finally, we evaluate all submissions on the surprise languages of Vietnamese, Lithuanian and Kazakh, not revealed to the participants until the conclusion of the shared task. The data is in the form of source–target translation pairs, with the source language always being English.

Size and splits: The multi-way parallel section of the corpus for our languages of interest consists of 34831 sentences. From this, we create training, validation and test sets of sizes 22204, 3919, and 8708 respectively by randomly sampling the original data.

3 Evaluation

Submission format: Participants were asked to submit indices of the top 20% of the training data (or 4440 sentences), corresponding to the best instances chosen by their systems. We then extract the source and target language sentences corresponding to the indices to prepare data files for MT models.

Model: We evaluate submissions by *finetuning* the mBART model (Liu et al., 2020) on the chosen instances. mBART is a multilingual denoising autoencoder trained on data from 25 languages, extracted from Common Crawl (Wenzek et al., 2020). We use the mbart-large-cc25 checkpoint from Facebook, which contains all 10 of our languages of interest in its pretraining data.

Training: We use the implementation and the default hyperparameters of mBART-large from the Huggingface hub (Wolf et al., 2020). All data is tokenized with the corresponding mBART-cc-25 sentence-piece tokenizer, and any empty lines on the source side are filtered out prior to training. We train each model for 20 epochs on a single nvidia V100 GPU, and use early-stopping based on validation set performance. We train five random runs of each model, and report the averaged score across all runs.

Baselines: We develop two baselines for comparing the submissions to, namely Random and Max. The random baseline randomly samples 20% of all instances from the training set. The max baseline sorts the English sentences in descending order by number of tokens, and selects the top 20%.

Metrics: All systems are evaluated with the chrF++ score (Popović, 2017), computed using the sacrebleu toolkit (Post, 2018).

4 Submissions

Two teams participated in the CoCo4MT 2023 shared task, under the team names `Williams` and `AST`. We describe their submissions below, and further details can be found in the system description papers attached to the proceedings.

4.1 Williams

The algorithm proposed by team `Williams`[3] is based on the idea of clustering training examples to find representative instances that can be chosen for training. Following Zhao et al. (2020), they highlight the importance of "balancing representativeness with redundancy", that is, making sure that the distribution of the training data is captured, without including multiple instances that are similar to each other. To achieve this objective, they use the SimCSE algorithm to obtain embeddings of each sentence in the training data, and then use cosine distance

[3]`https://github.com/Mark-Hopkins-at-Williams/coco4mt`

Language	Model	ChrF++ Score
Development languages		
Gujarati	Random	28.43
Gujarati	Max	25.62
Gujarati	Williams	29.59
Gujarati	AST	**29.80**
French	Random	52.16
French	Max	**54.75**
French	Williams	54.09
French	AST	53.38
Burmese	Random	37.11
Burmese	Max	39.75
Burmese	Williams	40.00
Burmese	AST	**40.13**
Test (Surprise) Languages		
Lithuanian	Random	42.65
Lithuanian	Max	**43.51**
Lithuanian	Williams	43.43
Lithuanian	AST	43.11
Kazakh	Random	31.45
Kazakh	Max	32.08
Kazakh	Williams	**33.16**
Kazakh	AST	32.30
Vietnamese	Random	45.13
Vietnamese	Max	44.85
Vietnamese	Williams	**45.68**
Vietnamese	AST	44.81

Table 1: Performances of all models on all development and test languages.

to compute the nearest neighbor of each sentence. They then iteratively select the sentence that is found to be the nearest neighbor of the most number of documents, until 20% of the original training data is selected. They report that this method out-performed other cluster based methods such as selecting cluster centroids.

4.2 AST

The algorithm proposed by team `AST`[4] is based on maximizing the information provided by each sentence, by selecting sentences that are the long, but also contain diverse sets of n-grams. They then greedily select sentences that optimize this objective. Additionally, they use the LaBSE model to compute sentence embeddings for each translation pair in the training set, and filter out sentences that have an LaBSE similarity score of less than 0.5. They also aim to filter out training instances that may potentially be mis-aligned. They do this by translating all English sentences to German and Indonesian using the mBART-50 model, and compute chrF++ scores for all instances. They discard sentences with a score below 20 as they may be misaligned, as well as sentences with a score above 60, as the information contained in them may already be well-represented in the pre-training data.

[4] `https://github.com/Mark-Hopkins-at-Williams/coco4mt`

Model	ChrF++ Score
Development Languages	
Random	39.22
Max	40.04
Williams	**41.22**
AST	41.10
Test (Surprise) Languages	
Random	39.74
Max	40.14
Williams	**40.75**
AST	40.07

Table 2: Average performance on the development and test languages.

5 Results

We first report the performance of all models on all languages in Table 1, that is, both the development languages released to the participants, and the surprise languages used for judging. On the development languages, we observe the highest scores for all models for French, which is very well represented in the mBART pre-training data with 9000M tokens, and also bears similarities to English. However, all models perform higher on Burmese than Gujarati, despite Gujarati having 140M tokens in CC25 while Burmese only has 56M tokens. We also see that both submissions outperform the baselines on the lower-resource languages of Gujarati and Burmese, but not on French. Although the `AST` system achieves the best performance on two development languages, on average, as seen in Table 2, the `Williams` submission performs best, with a score of 41.22, while the `AST` submission closely follows with an average score of 41.10.

On the test set of languages, or surprise languages, we see some similar trends. Highest performance for all models is seen on Vietnamese, which is the most prevalent in CC25 with 24000M tokens. Lithuanian, which has 1800M tokens comes next, and lowest performance is on Kazakh which has 476M tokens in the pretraining data. Although the max baseline outperforms both submissions on Lithuanian, the `Williams` system outperforms all other systems on all other languages. We further see that the performance of the `AST` submission is very close to the max baseline, potentially due to the submission also focusing on the longest sentences in its ranking. Finally, as seen in Table 2, the best performing system on average on the test languages is also the `Williams` system, which we officially judge as the winner of the shared task.

We highlight the fact that all three non-random methods described here are model-agnostic methods, that can identify instances with just access to parallel data and sentence embedding methods. The simple heuristic of choosing the longest sentences holds up well in comparison to more nuanced methods, even outperforming the others for Lithuanian. We leave it to future work to explore more advanced heuristics as well as develop model-specific methods to choose beneficial instances for machine translation.

6 Conclusion

In this overview paper, we presented the results of the first CoCo4MT 2023 shared task. The goal of the task was to discover methods to improve cost-efficiency of the machine translation annotation process, by identifying beneficial instances even without an existing parallel dataset. Participants were given access to data from four languages from the JHU Bible corpus to develop their algorithms, and three more languages to evaluate their systems. The task received two submissions, which were evaluated on three surprise or test languages. The winner of the shared task is the submission by team `Williams`, which clusters all training set instances, and selects representative examples while minimizing redundancies. We hope that the findings of this task will spur more research on improving annotation efficiency, particularly for low-resource languages.

References

Bhatnagar, R., Ganesh, A., and Kann, K. (2022). CHIA: CHoosing instances to annotate for machine translation. In *Findings of the Association for Computational Linguistics: EMNLP 2022*, pages 7299–7315, Abu Dhabi, United Arab Emirates. Association for Computational Linguistics.

Kim, Y., Graça, M., and Ney, H. (2020). When and why is unsupervised neural machine translation useless? In *Proceedings of the 22nd Annual Conference of the European Association for Machine Translation*, pages 35–44, Lisboa, Portugal. European Association for Machine Translation.

Koehn, P. (2005). Europarl: A parallel corpus for statistical machine translation. In *Proceedings of Machine Translation Summit X: Papers*, pages 79–86, Phuket, Thailand.

Lample, G., Conneau, A., Denoyer, L., and Ranzato, M. (2018). Unsupervised machine translation using monolingual corpora only. In *International Conference on Learning Representations*.

Liu, Y., Gu, J., Goyal, N., Li, X., Edunov, S., Ghazvininejad, M., Lewis, M., and Zettlemoyer, L. (2020). Multilingual denoising pre-training for neural machine translation. *Transactions of the Association for Computational Linguistics*, 8:726–742.

McCarthy, A. D., Wicks, R., Lewis, D., Mueller, A., Wu, W., Adams, O., Nicolai, G., Post, M., and Yarowsky, D. (2020). The Johns Hopkins University Bible corpus: 1600+ tongues for typological exploration. In *Proceedings of the Twelfth Language Resources and Evaluation Conference*, pages 2884–2892, Marseille, France. European Language Resources Association.

Popović, M. (2017). chrf++: words helping character n-grams. In *Proceedings of the second conference on machine translation*, pages 612–618.

Post, M. (2018). A call for clarity in reporting BLEU scores. In *Proceedings of the Third Conference on Machine Translation: Research Papers*, pages 186–191, Brussels, Belgium. Association for Computational Linguistics.

Wenzek, G., Lachaux, M.-A., Conneau, A., Chaudhary, V., Guzmán, F., Joulin, A., and Grave, E. (2020). CCNet: Extracting high quality monolingual datasets from web crawl data. In *Proceedings of the Twelfth Language Resources and Evaluation Conference*, pages 4003–4012, Marseille, France. European Language Resources Association.

Wolf, T., Debut, L., Sanh, V., Chaumond, J., Delangue, C., Moi, A., Cistac, P., Rault, T., Louf, R., Funtowicz, M., Davison, J., Shleifer, S., von Platen, P., Ma, C., Jernite, Y., Plu, J., Xu, C., Le Scao, T., Gugger, S., Drame, M., Lhoest, Q., and Rush, A. (2020). Transformers: State-of-the-art natural language processing. In *Proceedings of the 2020 Conference on Empirical Methods in Natural Language Processing: System Demonstrations*, pages 38–45, Online. Association for Computational Linguistics.

Zhao, Y., Zhang, H., Zhou, S., and Zhang, Z. (2020). Active learning approaches to enhancing neural machine translation. In *Findings of the Association for Computational Linguistics: EMNLP 2020*, pages 1796–1806, Online. Association for Computational Linguistics.

Williams College's Submission for the Coco4MT 2023 Shared Task

Alex Root asr6@williams.edu
Mark Hopkins mh24@williams.edu
Department of Computer Science, Williams College, Williamstown, MA, 01267

Abstract

Professional translation is expensive. As a consequence, when developing a translation system in the absence of a pre-existing parallel corpus, it is important to strategically choose sentences to have professionally translated for the training corpus. In our contribution to the Coco4MT 2023 Shared Task, we explore how sentence embeddings can be leveraged to choose an impactful set of sentences to translate. Based on six language pairs of the JHU Bible corpus, we demonstrate that a technique based on SimCSE embeddings outperforms a competitive suite of baselines.

1 Introduction

It has become increasingly possible to train decent translation models with small, high-quality parallel corpora. For instance, Maillard et al. (2023) recently showed that just 6000 professionally-translated sentences made a big impact on the quality of trained translation models for 39 low-resource languages.

This raises a research question. Suppose we want to develop a model that translates between a high-resource language and a low-resource language (or possibly a specialized domain of a moderately-resourced language). How should one select a "seed" dataset to have professionally translated from the high-resource language into the low-resource language? This is the subject of the Coco4MT 2023 Shared Task.

For our contribution to this shared task, we focus on *model-agnostic* approaches. In contrast to approaches that leverage model uncertainty to select sentences to professionally translate (Bhatnagar et al., 2022), model-agnostic approaches (Zhao et al., 2020) select a training corpus based exclusively on the distribution and content of sentences in the high-resource language. While ignoring model uncertainty may result in lower-quality data selection for a particular model, it has the potential advantage of broader applicability, as the data selection is not tied to a specific model architecture.

2 Task Description

Define a *translation model* t as a function that maps source-language documents to target-language documents. Each translation pair $(x, t(x))$ (where x is a source-language document) is assumed to have a non-negative real-valued quality $q(x, t(x))$. Given a distribution $P_{\mathcal{X}}$ over source-language documents, the quality of translation model t is the expected translation quality:

$$q(t) = E_{P_{\mathcal{X}}}[q(x, t(x))]$$

A *parallel corpus* is a set of pairs (x, y), where y is a target-language translation of source-language document x. A trainer τ takes a parallel corpus as its input, and outputs (possibly nondeterministically) a translation model t.

The Coco4MT 2023 Shared Task is about optimizing parallel corpus construction for training translation models. We have access to a monolingual corpus of documents $X = \{x_1, ..., x_n\}$ in a high-resource language, assumed to be drawn i.i.d. from document distribution $P_{\mathcal{X}}$. We also have access to a cost function $c : X \rightarrow \mathbb{R}^+$ that maps each document $x_i \in X$ to the positive real cost $c(x_i)$ of obtaining a professional translation for document x_i. For monolingual corpus X and a subset $I \subseteq \{1, ..., n\}$ of selected document ids, let $Z_{X,I} = \{(x_i, y_i) \mid i \in I\}$ be the parallel corpus we would obtain (i.e. y_i is the professional translation of document x_i) from commissioning translations for the documents associated with the selected ids. The cost of building parallel corpus $Z_{X,I}$ is therefore:

$$c(Z_{X,I}) = \sum_{i \in I} c(x_i)$$

The goal of the task is to construct a parallel corpus $Z_{X,I}$ that produces a translation model of maximal expected quality, subject to the constraint that the construction cost $c(Z_{X,I})$ is less than a specified budget B. In other words, we want to compute:

$$\hat{I} = \underset{\substack{I \subseteq \{1,...,n\}: \\ c(Z_{X,I}) \leq B}}{\text{argmax}} \; E[q(\tau(Z_{X,I}))]$$

where $E[q(\tau(Z_{X,I}))]$ is the expected quality of the translation model produced by trainer τ, when trained on parallel corpus $Z_{X,I}$.

The official Coco4MT 2023 Shared Task uses a uniform cost function, i.e. $c(x_i) = 1$ for all $x_i \in X$. In other words, all documents have the same translation cost. The budget $B = 0.2 * |X|$ is 20% of the documents in monolingual corpus X. We will also experiment with a token-based translation cost, i.e. where $c(x_i)$ equals the number of tokens in document x_i[1]. The corresponding budget B will be 20% of the tokens in corpus X.

3 Baselines

3.1 Simple Baselines

We experimented with three simple baselines:

- **longest**: choose ids corresponding to the longest documents in corpus X, until the budget is exhausted.
- **random**: choose ids uniformly at random, until the budget is exhausted.
- **weighted random**: choose ids from a categorical distribution where each document is weighted by token length, until the budget is exhausted.

3.2 Decay Logarithm Frequency (delfy)

As an additional baseline, we also implemented an algorithm from Zhao et al. (2020) called **de**cay **l**ogarithm **f**requenc**y** (**delfy**). The **delfy** algorithm attempts to choose a subset of documents that are *representative* of distribution $P_{\mathcal{X}}$ without being overly *redundant* (the intuition is that it is wasteful to commission translations of similar documents, even if these documents

[1] Since English is always the source language (and since punctuation arguably doesn't contribute to the translation cost of a sentence), we simply use whitespace-based tokenization in our experiments.

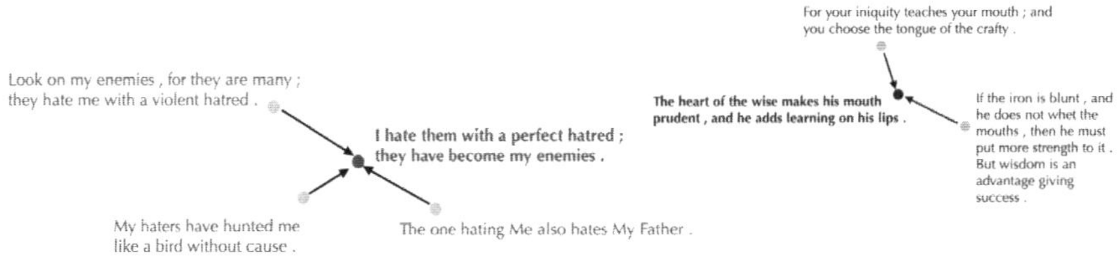

Figure 1: A visualization of our document selection approach. We embed each document using SimCSE (Gao et al., 2021) and then choose the most central documents to include in our training set.

are in a high-probability region of the document space). The **delfy** algorithm consists of K successive rounds of document selection, such that each round exhausts $\frac{1}{K}$ of the budget. During each round, the unselected documents are ranked according a formula that balances frequency in the overall corpus with infrequency in the documents selected during previous rounds. Then the top-ranked documents are selected. Following Zhao et al. (2020), we run $K = 20$ selection rounds. We refer the reader to Zhao et al. (2020) for details of the ranking formula.

4 Our Approach

Inspired by the **delfy** algorithm, we investigated other ways to balance representativeness with redundancy. Specifically, we focused on using document embeddings to select the documents to translate. Document embeddings seek to cluster documents based on lexical and semantic similarity. For instance, if we apply the popular document embedding model SimCSE (Gao et al., 2021) to the JHU Bible Corpus (McCarthy et al., 2020), we obtain clusters like the ones shown in Figure 1. For instance, the most similar sentence to *My haters have hunted me like a bird without cause* is *I hate them with a perfect hatred; they have become my enemies.*

The intuition behind our approach was to balance representativeness and redundancy by choosing representatives from each cluster of embeddings. We embedded each document using SimCSE (Gao et al., 2021), then determined the nearest neighbor (based on cosine similarity) of each document. In other words, we compiled the following set of document pairs:

$$\mathsf{nearest}(X) = \left\{ \left(x_i, \ \underset{x_j \in X \setminus \{x_i\}}{\text{argmin}} \ \mathsf{sim}(x_i, x_j) \right) \right\}$$

where $X = \{x_1, ...x_n\}$ is the high-resource language corpus (as defined in Section 2), and sim is the cosine similarity function. Then we ranked the high-resource documents based on how many times they were the nearest neighbor of another document:

$$\mathsf{centrality}(x_i) = \min(2, |\{(x_j, x_i) \in \mathsf{nearest}(X)\}|)$$

Based on this ranking, we selected documents from the high-resource corpus until the budget was exhausted. When using a uniform translation cost (i.e. when all documents had the same translation cost), ties were broken based on sentence length[2]. When using a token-based translation cost, ties were broken randomly.

We experimented with alternative approaches to selecting cluster representatives (e.g. centroids of k-nearest neighbor clustering), but these all underperformed the simple method described above.

[2]When two sentences had the same centrality, the longer sentence was preferred.

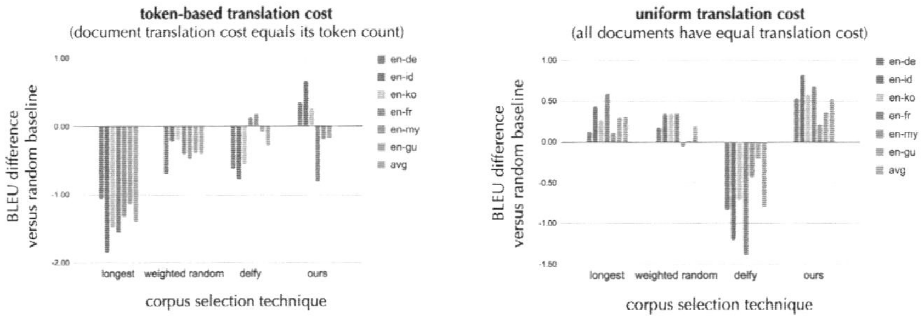

Figure 2: Results for token-based (left) and uniform (right) translation costs. For each language pair, we show the difference between the BLEU score of a model trained on documents selected by a given technique, versus a corresponding model trained on a randomly selected corpus. For each experiment, the budget is 20% of the high-resource training corpus (counted in terms of tokens and documents, respectively).

5 Experiments

We used the experimental setup provided by the Coco4LM 2023 Shared Task. The training corpus consisted of roughly 22k English sentences from the JHU Bible Corpus (McCarthy et al., 2020), along with translations in six other languages: German (de), Indonesian (id), Korean (ko), French (fr), Gujarati (gu), Burmese (my). Additionally, there was a development corpus of 3919 sentences and a test corpus of 8708 sentences (all from the biblical domain). Since none of the evaluated techniques used the non-English data for training[3], we evaluated on all six en-X language pairs (en-fr, en-gu, en-my, en-de, en-id, en-ko). For each corpus selection technique, we fine-tuned the mBART-50 model (Liu et al., 2020) on the documents[4] identified by that strategy and evaluated using BLEU (Papineni et al., 2002). We used the implementation and default parameters of mBART-50 provided by HuggingFace.

Results are shown in Figure 2. Our sentence embedding approach performed consistently across the two translation costs and six language pairs (with one exception: en-fr translation for the token-based translation cost). Surprisingly, the **delfy** algorithm consistently underperformed the random baseline, despite successes in other studies (Zhao et al., 2020). Perhaps this was due to the narrow domain (biblical) or the limited size of the training corpus.

6 Conclusion, Limitations, and Future Work

Sentence embeddings show potential as an instrument for selecting a good proxy dataset for a translation domain. However, it is important to acknowledge the limitations of this pilot study.

Domain Specificity: All conclusions were drawn on the basis of the JHU Bible Corpus.

Dataset Magnitude: All conclusions were drawn in the context of a 25k sentence corpus.

Budget: Our results are specific to a budget of 20% of the tokens/documents.

Sentence Embedding Method: We focused exclusively on SimCSE embeddings.

In future work, we would like to make more robust conclusions about our proposed technique by exploring a broader space of domains, dataset magnitudes, budgets, and sentence embeddings.

[3]The **delfy** algorithm used counts from the English corpus, and our approach used sentence embeddings from the English corpus.

[4]Most documents in this corpus were single sentences.

References

Bhatnagar, R., Ganesh, A., and Kann, K. (2022). CHIA: CHoosing instances to annotate for machine translation. In *Findings of the Association for Computational Linguistics: EMNLP 2022*, pages 7299–7315, Abu Dhabi, United Arab Emirates. Association for Computational Linguistics.

Gao, T., Yao, X., and Chen, D. (2021). SimCSE: Simple contrastive learning of sentence embeddings. In *Proceedings of the 2021 Conference on Empirical Methods in Natural Language Processing*, pages 6894–6910, Online and Punta Cana, Dominican Republic. Association for Computational Linguistics.

Liu, Y., Gu, J., Goyal, N., Li, X., Edunov, S., Ghazvininejad, M., Lewis, M., and Zettlemoyer, L. (2020). Multilingual denoising pre-training for neural machine translation. *Transactions of the Association for Computational Linguistics*, 8:726–742.

Maillard, J., Gao, C., Kalbassi, E., Sadagopan, K. R., Goswami, V., Koehn, P., Fan, A., and Guzman, F. (2023). Small data, big impact: Leveraging minimal data for effective machine translation. In *Proceedings of the 61st Annual Meeting of the Association for Computational Linguistics (Volume 1: Long Papers)*, pages 2740–2756, Toronto, Canada. Association for Computational Linguistics.

McCarthy, A. D., Wicks, R., Lewis, D., Mueller, A., Wu, W., Adams, O., Nicolai, G., Post, M., and Yarowsky, D. (2020). The Johns Hopkins University Bible corpus: 1600+ tongues for typological exploration. In *Proceedings of the Twelfth Language Resources and Evaluation Conference*, pages 2884–2892, Marseille, France. European Language Resources Association.

Papineni, K., Roukos, S., Ward, T., and Zhu, W.-J. (2002). Bleu: a method for automatic evaluation of machine translation. In *Proceedings of the 40th Annual Meeting of the Association for Computational Linguistics*, pages 311–318, Philadelphia, Pennsylvania, USA. Association for Computational Linguistics.

Zhao, Y., Zhang, H., Zhou, S., and Zhang, Z. (2020). Active learning approaches to enhancing neural machine translation. In *Findings of the Association for Computational Linguistics: EMNLP 2020*, pages 1796–1806, Online. Association for Computational Linguistics.

The AST Submission for the CoCo4MT 2023 Shared Task on Corpus Construction for Low-Resource Machine Translation

Steinþór Steingrímsson steinthor.steingrimsson@arnastofnun.is
The Árni Magnússon Institute for Icelandic Studies, Reykjavík, 107, Iceland

Abstract

We describe the AST submission for the CoCo4MT 2023 shared task. The aim of the task is to identify the best candidates for translation in a source data set with the aim to use the translated parallel data for fine-tuning the mBART-50 model. We experiment with three methods: scoring sentences based on n-gram coverage, using LaBSE to estimate semantic similarity and identify misalignments and mistranslations by comparing machine translated source sentences to corresponding manually translated segments in high-resource languages. We find that we obtain the best results by combining these three methods, using LaBSE and machine translation for filtering, and one of our n-gram scoring approaches for ordering sentences.

1 Introduction

Reliable parallel corpora are key to developing useful machine translation (MT) systems. Parallel corpora are commonly compiled by aligning corresponding documents in two or more languages on the sentence level, with the aim of pairing semantically equivalent segments in the languages. This can work well when source texts and translations of these texts are available. In cases where they are not available or not abundant, mining comparable corpora or web-scraped texts can be used to produce useful parallel pairs or to augment available parallel data. For some very low-resource (LR) language pairs or domains, neither parallel documents nor comparable corpora may be available, and in order to build an MT system that generates useful translation, creating a minimum set of training data by manually translating them may be necessary.

In scenarios where corpus creation for machine translation is carried out by translating sentences from a source language into a low-resource target language or in a specialized domain, it is important to use the annotation budget efficiently in order to come up with sentences that are likely to produce high-quality translations. In the CoCo4MT 2023 shared task, participants are to come up with ways to identify the best examples to translate from a high-resource (HR) source language, without any existing data in the target language. Translations of the source data are provided into a number of HR-languages and these translations can be used to help identify the best candidates for translation into the low-resource target language. A parallel corpus of 22,204 lines in English, German, Indonesian and Korean are provided. Participants can select up to 20% of these lines, with the corresponding pairs used to fine-tune an mBART model Liu et al. (2020), namely the mBART-50 (Tang et al., 2021). The winner of the shared task is the team whose instances result in the highest scoring model as measured by chrF++ (Popović, 2017).

Proceedings of the Second Workshop on Corpus Generation and Corpus Augmentation for Machine Translation, pages 33–38
September 5, 2023, Macau SAR, China.

2 Related Work

Parallel corpora compiled by aligning corresponding documents in two or more languages on the sentence level are available for a large number of language pairs, e.g. in the OPUS collection (Tiedemann, 2012). Ramesh et al. (2022) collect a combination of available parallel corpora and web-scraped material in a number of Indian languages. Bañón et al. (2020) collect web-scraped data, predominantly in the languages of the European Union and Bañón et al. (2022) aim to collect corpora for under-resourced European languages. For under-resourced languages unsupervised methods exploiting monolingual corpora have been applied (Lample et al., 2018; Artetxe et al., 2018), but have been found to need abundant monolingual data in similar domains, for the performance not to deteriorate (Marchisio et al., 2020).

Bhatnagar et al. (2022) present a system for choosing source language instances to annotate for MT. They find cross-lingual commonalities in instances that are useful for MT training and use these to identify instances for training a new language pair.

3 System Description

In selecting the best subset of segments using the HR-language pairs we consider sentence length, data diversity, misalignments and semantic equivalence. Our approaches are described in Section 3.2.

Before carrying out our experiments we did some preprocessing of the training, validation and test data sets.

3.1 Data Sets and Preprocessing

Participants in the shared task were provided access to parallel data from the JHU Bible corpus (McCarthy et al., 2020), in HR-languages to use for instance selection, and in LR-languages for evaluation of the data selection algorithms. The HR-languages were English, German, Korean and Indonesian, and the LR-languages were Gujarati, Burmese and French. Training, development and test splits for all languages, as well as baselines in the form of selected English instances, are made available in a GitHub repository for the shared task.[1]

The training files contain 22,204 lines, the test files are 8,708 lines and the development data comprise 3,919 lines. Upon inspection of the data we found that some lines contain empty strings in one or more of the HR-languages. We removed these empty lines from the English source file and deduplicated it, which gave us 19,718 lines to choose from. We also prepared our test and development data by removing all lines that were empty in one or more of the four HR-languages. This resulted in development files containing 3,410 lines and test files containing 7,622 lines. In our experiments, the development data are used for validation when fine-tuning the mBART-50 model on our selected training data sets and the test data for evaluating the usefulness of the data used in each experiment.

Data sets selected using two baseline methods are provided by the shared task organizers, one based on length and the other a random selection of sentences.

3.2 Experiments

Aiming to identify the instances in the training data that have the greatest potential to correctly inform an NMT system on how to correctly translate, we experimented with a number of approaches. Using the available HR-data, we evaluated our approaches on two translation directions: En→De and En→Id. We compare the results of our experiments to translations obtained by fine-tuning on the two baseline data sets. Our code is available on GitHub.[2]

[1] https://github.com/ananyaganesh/coco4mt-shared-task/

[2] https://github.com/steinst/coco4MT

Sentence length and diversity: In the task we are allowed a maximum number of sentences. Longer sentences should generally contain more information than shorter ones and should therefore be likely to give better results. One of the baselines is indeed a set of the 20% longest sentences in the source language, English. Instead of opting for a simple count of characters or tokens, we tokenize all source language sentences using the BPE-tokenization model used with mBART-50 and devise a greedy algorithm to try to order the sentences based on both length and diversity. The algorithm considers unigrams, bigrams and trigrams in the tokenized sentences and counts different such n-grams. In each round the highest scoring sentence is selected and removed from the pool of sentences. When previously selected sentences contain an n-gram for a set maximum number of times, it stops counting towards the score in the remaining sentences. Simplified pseudocode is given in Algorithm 1. We conduct three experiments, each having different number of allowed repetitions of each n-gram, with 1, 2 or 3 repetitions allowed.

Algorithm 1 Greedy Algorithm Selecting based on sentence length and n-gram diversity

$remaining\_lines = all\_source\_language\_lines$
$max\_ngrams = \{\}$
$allowed\_repetitions = n$
while $remaining\_lines \geq 1$ **do**
    for $line$ in $remaining\_lines$ **do**
        Count ngrams where (ngrams not in max_ngrams or $allowed\_repetitions \leq n$)
    end for
    $max\_ngrams \leftarrow$ ngrams from highest scoring line
    Remove highest scoring line from $remaining\_lines$
    Yield highest scoring line
end while

Semantic Similarity: When training MT systems we want the training data to contain accurate translations. LaBSE (Feng et al., 2022) is a model trained and optimized to produce similar representations for bilingual sentence pairs. It has been used for retrieving bitexts from parallel corpora. Feng et al. (2022) use it on its own for that purposes while Steingrímsson et al. (2021) use it as a part of a system that combines multiple approaches for the same purpose. It has been shown to be useful for scoring sentence pairs to identify possible faulty pairs that should be filtered out of an MT training set (Steingrímsson et al., 2023) and as a scoring mechanism for sentence alignment (Steingrímsson, 2023). In our experiments, we use LaBSE in combination with other approaches and remove all lines that obtain a LaBSE score under a given threshold for any of the three HR-language pairs with English is a source language. Feng et al. (2022) suggest that sentence pairs obtaining higher scores than 0.6 when mining comparable corpora can be useful for MT training. (Steingrímsson et al., 2023) experiment with using the scoring mechanism for multiple datasets and find that when working with data derived from parallel corpora, a lower threshold can be set. In our experiments we set a threshold to 0.5, with all sentence pairs obtaining lower scores being discarded.

Misalignments in the training data: Misalignments or partial misalignments in the training data can potentially have detrimental effects on the performance of MT systems (see e.g. Khayrallah and Koehn (2018)). To try to identify the most prominent misalignments we use the mBART-50 model, without any fine-tuning, to translate the English sentence pairs to German and Indonesian. For the HR-language pairs we expect to obtain translations that give a decent representation of the source sentences. We then calculate Chrf++ scores for each sentence pair

BLEU scores for two HR-language pairs		
Approach	EN→DE	EN→ID
Baseline: Longest Sentences	18.9	23.1
Baseline: Random Sentences	18.8	23.1
Greedy Algorithm - ngrams only count the first time (GA1)	17.4	23.4
Greedy Algorithm - First 2 occurrences of an ngram count (GA2)	18.4	26.0
Greedy Algorithm - First 3 occurrences of an ngram count (GA3)	18.2	25.9
GA1 + LaBSE and Chrf++ scores used for filtering LaBSE	18.4	23.0
GA2 + LaBSE and Chrf++ scores used for filtering LaBSE	21.3	26.2
GA3 + LaBSE and Chrf++ scores used for filtering LaBSE	17.9	23.6

Table 1: BLEU scores for different approaches.

and if the Chrf++ score is very low we assume there is a mismatch between the source and target sentences and remove these from our training data. On the other hand, if we achieve very high Chrf++ scores, we assume the contents of the sentence pairs are well represented in the training data and thus opt not to use these sentence pairs for training. We set the minimum threshold to 20.0 and maximum to 60.0.

Combinations of different methods: Finally, we try to combine our three approaches in various ways. The next section discusses the results for each of our approaches

4 Results and Discussion

We fine-tuned the mBART-50 model on the different datasets and selected the set of lines that obtained the highest BLEU score (Papineni et al., 2002) for English→German and English→Indonesian as evaluated on the cleaned test-set. Table 1 gives the results for the different approaches. We find that for English→German we only manage to beat the baseline instances once, while for English→Indonesian we do it all but once. There may be various reasons for this, one of them might be that the mBART-50 model is trained on large quantities of data in German, over 45M sentences Tang et al. (2021), and that our small parallel set is not enough to improve the translations to any extent. A lot less Indonesian data is used for training mBART-50, only 84k sentences, and thus a careful selection of parallel sentence pairs for fine-tuning may be more important in that case.

Our highest-scoring method uses the Chrf++ evaluation of translated sentences as well as a LaBSE threshold score to filter the datasets and remove lines that we deem more likely to be detrimental than others. We then order the remaining lines from highest to lowest scores obtained by running our greedy scoring algorithm and select the top 20% of the original number of lines, resulting in training sets of 4,440 lines for each language pair. This list of lines was submitted as our optimal list of instances for corpus construction.

5 Conclusion

We have described our approach to selecting 20% of the lines in a source language training set, for pairing with translations in other languages in order to obtain the optimal training data set from what is available. We find that our approach, as measured by BLEU to evaluate HR-language translation models, increases translation quality on the language that is not as well represented in the multilingual language model being fine-tuned. This may indicate that using only a low amount of data to fine-tune a model such as mBART-50 is more effective when the language is not well represented in the training data for the model.

References

Artetxe, M., Labaka, G., Agirre, E., and Cho, K. (2018). Unsupervised neural machine translation. In *International Conference on Learning Representations*.

Bañón, M., Chen, P., Haddow, B., Heafield, K., Hoang, H., Esplà-Gomis, M., Forcada, M. L., Kamran, A., Kirefu, F., Koehn, P., Ortiz Rojas, S., Pla Sempere, L., Ramírez-Sánchez, G., Sarrías, E., Strelec, M., Thompson, B., Waites, W., Wiggins, D., and Zaragoza, J. (2020). ParaCrawl: Web-Scale Acquisition of Parallel Corpora. In *Proceedings of the 58th Annual Meeting of the Association for Computational Linguistics*, pages 4555–4567, Online. Association for Computational Linguistics.

Bañón, M., Esplà-Gomis, M., Forcada, M. L., García-Romero, C., Kuzman, T., Ljubešić, N., van Noord, R., Sempere, L. P., Ramírez-Sánchez, G., Rupnik, P., Suchomel, V., Toral, A., van der Werff, T., and Zaragoza, J. (2022). MaCoCu: Massive collection and curation of monolingual and bilingual data: focus on under-resourced languages. In *Proceedings of the 23rd Annual Conference of the European Association for Machine Translation*, pages 303–304, Ghent, Belgium. European Association for Machine Translation.

Bhatnagar, R., Ganesh, A., and Kann, K. (2022). CHIA: CHoosing instances to annotate for machine translation. In *Findings of the Association for Computational Linguistics: EMNLP 2022*, pages 7299–7315, Abu Dhabi, United Arab Emirates. Association for Computational Linguistics.

Feng, F., Yang, Y., Cer, D., Arivazhagan, N., and Wang, W. (2022). Language-agnostic BERT Sentence Embedding. In *Proceedings of the 60th Annual Meeting of the Association for Computational Linguistics (Volume 1: Long Papers)*, pages 878–891, Dublin, Ireland. Association for Computational Linguistics.

Khayrallah, H. and Koehn, P. (2018). On the Impact of Various Types of Noise on Neural Machine Translation. In *Proceedings of the 2nd Workshop on Neural Machine Translation and Generation*, pages 74–83, Melbourne, Australia. Association for Computational Linguistics.

Lample, G., Conneau, A., Denoyer, L., and Ranzato, M. (2018). Unsupervised machine translation using monolingual corpora only. In *International Conference on Learning Representations*.

Liu, Y., Gu, J., Goyal, N., Li, X., Edunov, S., Ghazvininejad, M., Lewis, M., and Zettlemoyer, L. (2020). Multilingual denoising pre-training for neural machine translation. *Transactions of the Association for Computational Linguistics*, 8:726–742.

Marchisio, K., Duh, K., and Koehn, P. (2020). When does unsupervised machine translation work? In *Proceedings of the Fifth Conference on Machine Translation*, pages 571–583, Online. Association for Computational Linguistics.

McCarthy, A. D., Wicks, R., Lewis, D., Mueller, A., Wu, W., Adams, O., Nicolai, G., Post, M., and Yarowsky, D. (2020). The Johns Hopkins University Bible corpus: 1600+ tongues for typological exploration. In *Proceedings of the Twelfth Language Resources and Evaluation Conference*, pages 2884–2892, Marseille, France. European Language Resources Association.

Papineni, K., Roukos, S., Ward, T., and Zhu, W.-J. (2002). BLEU: A Method for Automatic Evaluation of Machine Translation. In *Proceedings of the 40th Annual Meeting of the Association for Computational Linguistics*, pages 311–318, Philadelphia, Pennsylvania. Association for Computational Linguistics.

Popović, M. (2017). chrF++: words helping character n-grams. In *Proceedings of the Second Conference on Machine Translation*, pages 612–618, Copenhagen, Denmark. Association for Computational Linguistics.

Ramesh, G., Doddapaneni, S., Bheemaraj, A., Jobanputra, M., AK, R., Sharma, A., Sahoo, S., Diddee, H., J, M., Kakwani, D., Kumar, N., Pradeep, A., Nagaraj, S., Deepak, K., Raghavan, V., Kunchukuttan, A., Kumar, P., and Khapra, M. S. (2022). Samanantar: The Largest Publicly Available Parallel Corpora Collection for 11 Indic Languages. *Transactions of the Association for Computational Linguistics*, 10:145–162.

Steingrímsson, S., Loftsson, H., and Way, A. (2023). Filtering matters: Experiments in filtering training sets for machine translation. In *Proceedings of the 24th Nordic Conference on Computational Linguistics (NoDaLiDa)*, pages 588–600, Tórshavn, Faroe Islands. University of Tartu Library.

Steingrímsson, S., Lohar, P., Loftsson, H., and Way, A. (2021). Effective Bitext Extraction From Comparable Corpora Using a Combination of Three Different Approaches. In *Proceedings of the 14th Workshop on Building and Using Comparable Corpora (BUCC 2021)*, pages 8–17, Online (Virtual Mode). INCOMA Ltd.

Steingrímsson, S. (2023). *Effectively compiling parallel corpora for machine translation in resource-scarce conditions*. PhD thesis, Reykjavik University.

Tang, Y., Tran, C., Li, X., Chen, P.-J., Goyal, N., Chaudhary, V., Gu, J., and Fan, A. (2021). Multilingual translation from denoising pre-training. In *Findings of the Association for Computational Linguistics: ACL-IJCNLP 2021*, pages 3450–3466, Online. Association for Computational Linguistics.

Tiedemann, J. (2012). Parallel data, tools and interfaces in OPUS. In *Proceedings of the Eighth International Conference on Language Resources and Evaluation (LREC'12)*, pages 2214–2218, Istanbul, Turkey. European Language Resources Association (ELRA).

Author Index